# I Will Be
# the Woman He Loved

## Learning to Live Again
## on the Thames Path

### A Memoir

Advance Praise for *I Will Be the Woman He Loved*

"I laughed, I cried, I cheered for Tania and her indomitable spirit. *I Will Be the Woman He Loved* deftly balances the expectations (or lack thereof) of a woman in a man's world and her commitment to the man who was her world as they face the unimaginable, hand in hand. It is a funny, poignant, and sometimes sad—but always optimistic—story about resilience, love, and living life one step at a time."

—Kimberley Lovato, travel journalist
and author, *Pisa Loves Bella*


"Romanov turns a many-days hike along an English river into a metaphor for life. We all perhaps live many lives, but Romanov's surely pushes that trope to the limit. From her birth in a country that no longer exists, through her family's flight to a country that no longer exists, through a refugee camp in post-war Italy, to an ostracized immigrant childhood in San Francisco, to a trailblazing role as a hotshot young female tech executive in a notoriously male-dominated industry, and on to a marriage with the love of her life, the soulmate with whom she hikes the world's highest mountains. It is his untimely death that launches the bereaved widow on her hike along the Thames, chronicled so candidly in this poignant memoir, wherein Romanov transforms grief into meaning."

—Tamim Ansary, author
*The Invention of Yesterday* and *Destiny Disrupted*

"The thread tying together Romanov's story is the determination to be herself—a theme to which many, if not all, of us can relate. Like her, a professional woman before there were many of us in positions of power, I found it both moving and inspiring—and at times funny—to see lessons from that period revisited for our post-#MeToo era. Ultimately, Romanov's tale reminds us that no matter the challenge, including devastating loss, we always have the choice to reinvent ourselves and throw ourselves fully into whatever is next."

—Eva Auchincloss, former executive director
Women's Sports Foundation


"As she treks beside the meandering Thames, Tania Romanov maneuvers the powerful rapids of excruciating grief with courage and grace, propelled by nature, music, and memories of a deep love. She's accompanied by friends, but inside Tania the 'hollow ache of an absence' persists. This is the inspiring story, told in her trademark honest and refreshing prose, of how she transforms loss into a presence that ultimately guides her way forward and endures."

—Erin Byrne, author
*Wings: Gifts of Art, Life, and Travel in France*


"*I Will Be the Woman He Loved* is a multifaceted love story that poignantly recounts not only the love Romanov shared with her soulmate, Harold, but her unique love of people and her unfaltering love of life. Told over the course of a long walk with two women friends, Tania's experience calls to mind a beloved Chinese proverb: when three people walk together, there is always a teacher among them. Indeed, Tania's walk proves to be full of insights and lessons as she revisits the past and struggles to envision a new future in the wake of devastating loss. Told with poetic interludes of language that are both melodic and powerful, *I Will Be the Woman He Loved* is a book to which every woman—single, married, divorced, or widowed—can relate."

—The Hon. Julie M. Tang,
retired San Francisco Superior Court Judge


"*I Will Be the Woman He Loved* is a vivid and transportive description of Romanov's walk with two women friends through England—cold, rainy, dark, filled with choral music and ancient towns. Their journey is woven with love, loss, heartbreak, and survival. It left me with an overwhelming sense that a great love lives forever. It expands us in unimaginable ways as we see through Tania. A must read."

—Saumya Roy, author
*Castaway Mountain*


"The death of your partner—your soulmate—drains your life, leaving an indescribable loss. You come to realize that loss is not just for the one who has left this life, but also for the self you no longer know how to define or be. Tania doesn't have answers, so she does what she knows how to do best: she walks. She sets out on the Thames Path and, as her feet propel her along the trail one step at a time, her mind also begins to find a familiar rhythm. An enjoyable read that offers adventure and hope."

—Ann Miller, former TV executive
and Emmy Award-winning executive producer

"*I Will Be the Woman He Loved* is a delightful book, one full of experiences, feelings, personal grief and growth. I highly recommend this book for everyone, but especially travelers and would-be travelers, and those facing the loss of loved ones."

—Judith Hamilton, former CEO
Classroom Connect and Dataquest
author, *Animal Expressions*

# I Will Be
# the Woman He Loved

## Learning to Live Again
## on the Thames Path

A Memoir

Tania Romanov
with Matthew Félix

solificatio

San Francisco, California

*I Will Be the Woman He Loved*
*Learning to Live Again on the Thames Path*
*A Memoir*

Copyright © 2024
by Tania Romanov Amochaev and Matthew Félix
All rights reserved.

First Published by Solificatio
San Francisco, California
2024

ISBN: 979-8-9858781-5-8

Modified "Thames Path route sketch.png" by MartinD licensed under Creative Commons Attribution-Share Alike 4.0 International license (https://creativecommons.org/licenses/by-sa/4.0/deed.en)

Cover and interior book design by Solificatio
www.solificatio.com

To Harold, with all my love

## Contents

Author Note ..................................................................xiii
Prologue.......................................................................xv
Part One: Walking Together ..........................................1
  1. Grief..................................................................3
  2. A Seed Planted ................................................7
  3. Marital Status..................................................9
  4. And Then There Were Three.........................20
  5. Not Quite a Plan............................................23
  6. It's Cold Out There .......................................26
  7. A Routine Exam.............................................28
  8. Voice of an Angel ..........................................32
  9. Bridges ...........................................................43
  10. Three's Company..........................................50
  11. Russian Easter ...............................................57
  12. Food and Drink ............................................64
  13. One Question ...............................................68
  14. Reinvention...................................................79
  15. Staggered Maturities.....................................89
  16. Curiosity .....................................................105
  17. Condition of Entry .....................................117
  18. A New Woman............................................129
  19. Never Say Goodbye .....................................155
  20. No Regrets ..................................................158
  21. Always Here ................................................168

22. Better than Goodbye .................................................. 175
Part Two: Walking Alone ................................................. 181
    23. Oversharing ......................................................... 183
    24. A Loose Woman .................................................. 189
    25. Breaking with the Past ........................................ 199
    26. Bridge to Love .................................................... 206
    27. Lunch ................................................................. 227
    28. The Thames Barrier ............................................ 231
    29. Bhutan ................................................................ 238
Part Three: After the Walk .............................................. 255
    30. A House is Not a Home ...................................... 257
    31. Just Say Yes ........................................................ 261
    32. Two is Better than One ...................................... 266
Epilogue ........................................................................... 269
Memorial Talk ................................................................. 273
About the Authors .......................................................... 278

# Author Note

This memoir depicts a lifetime of actual events recounted as truthfully as possible, based on recollections of the author and persons mentioned herein. When necessary, dialogue has been recreated and narrative details supplemented by research. Some names and identifying details have been changed out of privacy considerations. An earlier version of the chapter "Bhutan" appeared in the author's travel collection, *Never a Stranger*.

# Prologue

"What was he like, your husband?"

I was in London, sitting on a bench along the Thames. A light breeze off the river had prompted me to zip up my coat, my hands grateful for deep pockets. Behind me cars flew by in a steady stream, the air tainted in their wake. Branches lay bare overhead, seagulls glided across a gray sky. I felt relaxed—until asked the question.

The woman feeding the birds paused and looked at me. Her puffy cheeks were rosy, her clear blue eyes bright like someone decades younger. The glasses she wore suggested otherwise, as did defined—though not unattractive—lines mapping the contours of her face. As she brushed away one of her silvery locks, expectant, her expression betrayed no sense of indiscretion.

Worried what else I might share, I blurted something about how "wonderful" my husband had been, excused myself, and continued my stroll.

After a week of walking with two close friends, I needed to be alone. Or so I had thought. I must have been desperate, telling a complete stranger that I was a recent widow.

I had lost my husband Harold to the prostate cancer he battled for half of our relationship. One day I was the busy CEO of a technology company; the next he and I were traveling the world, doing all those things you hope to do when your loved one's days are numbered.

Harold had been given a year-and-a-half survival prognosis, making every day he held on a gift to be savored. All the better when we found ourselves with many more of them than expected, as, year by year, Harold confounded the experts. It would be fifteen years before we were eventually told he had six months to live.

Five days later he was gone.

I haven't researched it, but I believe that after his death I suffered something like post-traumatic stress disorder, or PTSD. For years I had battled a relentless enemy determined to take away my loved one. When he disappeared, I was in shock: I lost the centerpiece around which my world revolved.

I craved him with a hunger nothing could fill. At the same time, not unlike after college, I found myself trying to figure out what life was all about.

And what was next.

# Part One:
# Walking Together

# Grief

For me, Harold was many things.

But there were two things he was not.

The first was his body. It was ruined. He was no longer in it, the body that held and protected him for seventy-one years, four months, ten days, and I don't know how many hours and minutes. Now that ravaged body had let him go.

The second thing was the medical paraphernalia. It suffocated me. It kept me from feeling, from owning my space. I had to be free of it.

While perfect strangers took Harold's body away, I left the house and walked the short distance to his redwood grove, several trees of which he was especially fond. Looking up at their towering trunks and widespread branches, I took a seat on the spongey mat of their fallen needles and waited. Dear friends removed the cushioned toilet seat, changed the bed linens, and carried thousands of pills and liquids to the shed. They removed all traces of the illness that Harold had fought. And now lost.

By the time I could bear to walk back into my house—what had been *our* house—only friends and family remained. And an enormous void. A confusing mix, in which we shared an evening of eating and reminiscing.

The next day I called to have the bed taken away. The king-size adjustable bed that guaranteed a good night's rest or

## I Will Be the Woman He Loved

your money back, the third bed in three months, the last in a futile attempt to ease Harold's discomfort.

"What's wrong with the bed?" asked the voice on the phone.

"It's too big now."

Silence.

"OK," the woman eventually said, "we'll pick it up next week and bring out a new queen one. Does that work for you?"

"Unfortunately, it does."

Some weeks after Harold died, I got a book on grief.

The first pages caught me short, as though speaking directly to my own experience. Planning for and attending the memorial. The celebration afterwards: a house full of friends and relatives, the food they brought, the memories they shared against a backdrop of music. And how when it ended—just like the book said—they all went away, but the dead person stayed dead.

I relived that shock every time I came home.

Harold always stayed dead.

I stopped reading the book and never opened it again. Not it nor any of the other books about grief friends gave me, hoping to help.

One day I sat at the computer in my study, looking at the website where so many people poured out memories of Harold. My eyes brimmed over. Rather than resist, I let the tears flow. For the first time since the memorial, I cried.

Soon I was howling.

I thought I was going to die. Emotion surged from my gut with a force I wasn't sure I could bear, my abdomen contracting, the air squeezed from my lungs, tears cascading like rain falling so hard it makes a windshield opaque. I gasped again and again, at the mercy of my convulsions.

Before I knew it, I was on the floor, incapacitated by an unbearably sharp pain near my belly. It took all the energy I had to curl into a fetal position, pushing back into place what doctors would later diagnose as a suspected hernia.

And then the tears stopped.

"Never again," I swore to myself, catching my breath and wiping away the last of them. "Never again."

Maybe others could find healing through tears. Weeping as a form of mourning was not for me. Even when it didn't result in a hernia, it was too painful. It didn't move me forward.

It never happened again.

Instead I opted for a strategy akin to managing income taxes: minimize and avoid them as long as possible within the law, in the hope and expectation that the future will reduce them, either through lower rates or higher means.

So, too, I believed, dealing with the pain of Harold's loss would get easier with time. For now, I would not give into self-pity, self-analysis, or crying jags.

Over coffee one day, my neighbor, Mary, shared how she responded when people sometimes asked if she ever thought of her husband Jack, who had died unexpectedly four years before Harold.

"I tell them I don't think there was a moment in the

first years after his death that he wasn't on my mind. Not a single moment."

I was stunned. She was right.

It wouldn't be until one afternoon years after Harold was gone that I would unexpectedly look up from my journal and be astonished to realize, "I haven't thought of Harold all day."

# A Seed Planted

It was mid-January 2012, eight months since Harold's death, and I was in the woods mushrooming with my friend Sue. She was a novice. After twenty years exploring the forests behind my house in Sonoma County, California, I was a relative expert.

It was a year of early mushrooming promise. September rains had led to late-October chanterelles, a full month ahead of schedule. But the rains had since become sporadic, and we spent more time that morning tramping and talking than finding mushrooms.

As we talked about our passion for walking, I told Sue about the Himalayan treks and so many others that Harold and I had loved. I shared stories from one of our last outings, through the Moroccan desert with two young nomads and their three camels. Walking is always healing for me, as it was for Harold.

Since his death, I had been spending a lot of time in San Francisco, where I grew up. I walked the streets, the hills, the beaches. I fell in love all over again with my favorite city, walking until I was exhausted beyond thinking. I walked until there was little room left for emotion. I walked until I was numb.

"John and I also love to walk!"

Sue's exclamation brought me back to the present.

Her husband John rarely joined our mostly female walking group. Harold, on the other hand, had been such a regular that we had often joked that our group consisted of

"Harold and his harem."

"In fact," Sue continued, "we do a major walk on every significant anniversary. We're walking across Scotland this year for our tenth."

"What were some of the other walks?" I wondered.

"Well, for our fifth we walked the Thames Path from Windsor to Oxford."

"Really?" I asked, surprised I'd never heard them talk about it. "How long a walk was it?"

"I think we were on the trail for ten days," Sue recalled, adding that she couldn't remember how they got the idea and that they had planned very little in advance. An avid rower, once she learned that the trail went through Henley, site of a world-famous annual regatta, it was a done deal.

We stumbled onto our first chanterelle, and all thoughts of England disappeared—until a few days later. When Sue returned my mushrooming bag, she brought with her the Cicerone guide to the Thames Path.

The seed was planted.

# Marital Status

The evening after my outing with Sue, I decided to cook a mushroom feast for my improbable new roommates.

Pat and Frank had been staying in my downstairs guest suite since October, when their home renovation hit a major snag. Inviting them to stay was a sure sign that I had definitively left behind the Tania I had known so well for so long. The Tania married to Harold for thirty years would no sooner have invited guests to live downstairs than she would have had a root canal without anesthesia. But this Tania, this post-Harold blank slate, welcomed them without a second thought.

I am an intensely private person. I love being with people, but I recharge by being alone. I rarely travel with others because I worry about feeling trapped. Harold was the exception: being with him was as comfortable as being by myself.

As I gathered Christmas cards in the way of setting the table, I reopened a card from my old friend Linda. Three words over a picture of her with her daughter and son broke me up: "I'm single again."

The first time I opened the card, I had been oblivious to her note, just as I had been oblivious to much of what occurred the previous six months. Now the words glared at me like a guilty conscience. How could I be so self-obsessed and uncaring?

In the late 1970s I was the youngest general manager and almost assuredly the only female division head at

Control Data, a multi-billion-dollar computer company in Minneapolis. Linda had completed a PhD in psychology at the University of Minnesota but, after an eleven-year career in special education, decided to go into business. She researched executives in local companies and set up more than a hundred interviews, including one with me.

I was immediately drawn to this dynamic and attractive woman. She was tall and slender, with dark hair framing a face that exuded confidence. Even when she smiled, her eyes pierced mine and made it clear: she was on a mission, determined to forge her own future. About my age, in her early thirties, she was smart, independent, and knew what she wanted. She wasn't going to let much stand in her way.

We became fast friends, supporting each other through our respective relationship ups and downs. When I went through my tumultuous two-year courtship with Harold, Linda was there for me every step of the way.

After Harold and I married, Linda got into a wonderful relationship with Terry, who moved from Albuquerque and launched a private therapy practice in Minneapolis. After they married, she was able to balance her successful business career with the births of their daughter and son. Terry and Linda bought a house on Lake Minnetonka, were active in their church, and shared child-rearing responsibilities. It seemed they had the perfect life.

A few years after Harold and I moved to California, Linda came to visit. Over ruby-red glasses of an earthy local pinot, she and I caught up on the deck of our home in Healdsburg, nestled in the redwoods and overlooking the Russian River Valley.

"I envy you and Harold. Your relationship seems so

## Walking Together

open and easy," she commented, inhaling the aroma of the wine before taking a sip.

"It feels like that now," I said, my own glass approaching my lips. "But remember the early days? How impossible it seemed that we would ever get our issues resolved?"

"Oh my god," Linda said, her eyes growing larger, as though she still couldn't believe it, even all these years later. "You guys went back and forth and back and forth!"

"You got that right!" I laughed. "He couldn't decide whether or not to get a divorce. I couldn't decide whether or not to get married."

"And how many times did you break up? I think I finally lost count!"

"Six!" I said. "But we could never resist getting back together."

"Maybe, but that didn't stop you from kicking him out of the house!"

We both burst into laughter.

It happened during an otherwise romantic fireside evening.

Our passion every bit as hot as the flames, little could we have known a single spark was about to set off a whole other inferno.

"I'm just not sure what to do," Harold confessed, as we caught our breath, the smell of burning wood heavy on the air.

"What?" I demanded. "Seriously, after all we've talked about, you're still not sure! Are you kidding me?"

"It's not her, it's the kids," he beseeched. "I just don't know if I can leave them."

I'd heard it all before. Yet I could not believe my ears—and I didn't want to listen to another word.

"Well, you're leaving now!" I howled, jumping to my feet and gesturing to the door.

"What? It's the middle of the night! I—"

"Out!" I commanded, my face like one possessed, shape-shifting in the flickering red-orange hues.

"But, honey, let's just—"

My piercing gaze cut him short. He knew better.

"Fine!" he shouted, buttoning his shirt and looking for his glasses, before getting to his feet.

"And don't call me until you've finally made up your mind!" I hollered out the front door.

A light went on at the neighbors'. A curtain moved in their window. Harold bounded down the front yard's long flight of stairs.

"I don't plan on calling you at all!" he shouted from the street, as he searched for his keys.

"It's not her, it's the kids," rang in my ears as I slammed the door. He might not have wanted to admit it, but the truth was that both continued to be issues.

Harold's first wife came from a prominent family, had worked in Asia and traveled extensively, and exuded confidence. During their courtship and newlywed stages, they seemed a match made in heaven. As time wore on, during which they had a son, Brad, and a daughter, Beth, fractures in their marriage suggested otherwise. Eventually, there was no denying it: they weren't compatible as life partners.

Now he was with another woman who presented herself as strong and independent, leaving him torn between two conflicting fears. If we got married, would time reveal incompatibilities that had yet to surface? Would I turn out to be dependent, like some women who had crossed his path? Or, possibly worse, would I prove to be as strong as I seemed—and too much for him to handle?

I had already given him reason to doubt.

Harold and I hadn't been dating for long when I invited him to my house.

When the time came to make dinner, I turned toward the kitchen. As I did, something didn't feel right. Looking over my shoulder, I saw Harold taking a seat on the living-room couch.

Scarcely had his derrière made contact with the cushion than I asked, "You don't think I'm going into the kitchen *alone*, do you?"

Caught off guard, he sat up straight.

"Aren't *you* cooking?" he asked, as though apologizing, if not arguing his defense.

"I don't do anything alone in the kitchen," I explained, savoring each word like bites of the meal we were about to make—together.

"Oh," Harold choked, trying to digest both his faux pas and the sudden notice of what was expected of him. "But I don't know how to do anything in the kitchen."

"What a gift!" I exclaimed, clapping my hands as though genuinely overcome by joy. "You get to learn!"

If the man could get an MBA from Stanford, he could chop a few onions.

From that day forward we always cooked together. We did the dishes together, too—I washed, he dried. In the kitchen, we did everything together.

In the unlikely event Harold had any lingering doubts our relationship would not be defined by traditional gender roles, an episode on our first trip lay them definitively to rest.

We had just landed in Utah, where we were going skiing. After we deplaned and got our luggage, we proceeded to the rental agency to pick up our car.

"Where are the keys?" I asked, once we had completed the paperwork and left behind the rental counter.

"I have them," Harold replied, rows of vehicles stretching out before us as we entered the bitter-cold garage. It smelled of dust, grease, and exhaust. A short distance away tires screeched as they turned on concrete.

"Why do *you* have the keys?" I demanded, my roller bag in tow.

"Well, I rented the car," Harold responded, choosing his words carefully. He knew better than to confess "because I'm the guy."

"What difference does it make who rented the car?"

"If I rented the car, don't I drive?" he asked, holding his ground.

"If we're taking a car, we both drive," I pronounced.

Without another word, he handed me the keys.

I was pleased the conversation had gone so well, that Harold hadn't put up any resistance. What I didn't know at the time was that he hated to drive. Although he kept a straight face, my insistence on being behind the wheel could hardly have made him happier. I became the driver not only then but going forward, freeing him to focus exclusively on navigation, a role he loved and in which I had little interest.

The morning after my fireside dispute with Harold, the neighbors and I appeared on our doorsteps in unwelcome unison. A well-off middle-aged couple with grown kids, they still got up at the crack of dawn. He carried a briefcase. She was holding a tennis racket, her hair pulled into a ponytail.

I paused. The lawns separating our homes were big. But not that big.

Gretchen paused, too, shooting a look at Pete. Despite the distance, I could have sworn I saw the trace of a smirk, as though they were sharing an inside joke. Before I could say anything, she did.

"Rough night?"

"Oh god Gretchen, I'm so sorry." I felt like a highschooler caught throwing a party.

"Not as sorry as he is, I bet!" Pete joked, before they headed to their car.

It was funny looking back on it with Linda. But at the time, punishing Harold for his indecision hadn't been entirely fair. While by that point in our relationship my mind was made up, that hadn't always been the case. For a long time, my own past relationship trauma made me question whether I ever wanted to get married.

I had just graduated from Berkeley and taken a job as a programmer for a super-computer company in what is now Silicon Valley. Greg was a year older, from a comfortably well-off family. A "true American," as I still classified people in those days, like his parents he was a tennis player.

A poor immigrant girl driven to prove my worth, I

spent the summer working and getting ready for our September nuptials. A relaxed, handsome guy with few worries, he planned to work with his father and eventually take over the family business. He spent his summer traveling in Europe, playing the amateur tennis circuit.

Upon his return two weeks before the wedding, he delivered devastating news: he couldn't go through with it. He wasn't ready to get married. The rug I had been walking to the altar was yanked out from under me, and I found myself in a free fall.

While ours wasn't necessarily a match made in heaven, we had been together more than five years. Whenever we tried to split up, we couldn't bear to be apart. Didn't that mean we were meant to be together?

Apparently not.

My parents had taught me to steel myself against external forces that could ruin life, like wars had done to theirs. They didn't want me left with nothing at age thirty, forced to start over. But they had also taught me I could count on family and the people close to me. I had wrongly assumed that included Greg.

It was terrifying to learn that nothing in life could be relied on, not even the boy—now man—with whom I had shared my virginity; who stood by me when our very first act of love resulted in pregnancy, followed by a highly illegal abortion across the border from El Paso; who abandoned his previous European tennis tour when I ran into serious difficulties at a summer job in Hawaii, flying to be there for me without being asked.

None of that mattered. Our relationship was over in an instant. The wedding invitations were rescinded, the gifts returned. My family, who had been dubious about the whole thing but supported me nonetheless, discovered they were right all along.

Publicly humiliated, my soul crushed, every aspect of my life thrown into catastrophic upheaval, the pain was nearly unbearable. I wasn't sure I even wanted to keep on living. More than one night I went to bed wishing never to wake up.

With time, I got over it. I convinced myself that Greg and I weren't right for each other after all. I needed to prove myself, and I couldn't marry the first man I had seriously dated. Not only would I be OK, but this was the best thing that could have happened to me.

I swore I would never, ever put myself into a situation where my emotional and mental well-being depended on someone else, where a mere change of their heart could cause me such devastation and trauma, turning my world upside-down.

I would never be so vulnerable again.

"God, I didn't know all that, Tania," Linda commented, letting the Greg debacle sink in.

"Well, you know," I joked, trying to lighten the mood, "it's not a story I tend to lead with."

"Now that I know what you went through, I'm amazed you ever got married at all!"

As Linda and I went on reminiscing, I couldn't ignore a gut feeling that something wasn't right. Soon the feeling was so strong I had to give it voice.

"We've talked about my marriage, but you haven't said anything about yours," I pointed out. "Is everything OK?"

Linda fell silent, tears filling her eyes.

"It's not good, Tania. In fact, I don't actually have a marriage. Terry is abusive. He refuses to get a job. The marriage counseling wasn't working, and I can barely stomach the thought of going home—but I want to be with my children."

I could hardly believe my ears.

"Are they all right?" I asked, the grip on my glass tightening.

"Oh, yes. It's not physical abuse," Linda insisted, "but he torments me verbally."

"Oh dear, Linda. What are you going to do?"

My heart was breaking. I wanted to do something—*anything*—to help.

"I need to figure out how to move on. I wish we'd fought before we got married, so I could have seen that side of him," she lamented.

We both took a drink, our thoughts filling the painful silence.

Eventually she did leave him, rebuilding her life around her church, career, and daughter and son, who grew into lovely adults. And although over the past couple of years we had mostly lost touch, I knew she had recently remarried, to a prominent surgeon at the Mayo Clinic.

But now this Christmas card.

I called her the next day.

Linda explained what had happened. After a trial period commuting to and from Rochester, where Mayo is located, she had sold her house to join her husband. No sooner had she done so than things fell apart.

During their brief courtship, Terry had feigned interest in Linda's liberal, social-justice church and watching

CNN. Immediately after the nuptials, she learned he was a member of a conservative, Evangelical church and watched FOX News three to four hours a day. When they travelled to the Galápagos Islands, she learned he didn't believe in evolution.

All that withstanding, they hadn't divorced and, in theory at least, were still trying to sort out their relationship.

Because she was putting two kids through college and graduate school, respectively, Linda needed to maintain her income. She was serving on corporate boards, consulting, and teaching. Having "retired" at Terry's urging after their marriage, she was also considering a return to full-time employment.

We talked about getting together, but Minneapolis was not on my agenda anytime soon, nor was California on hers.

An unexpected possibility presented itself when she mentioned she was heading to a board meeting in Denmark in February, stopping in London on the way.

"What do you think about a walk in England?" I asked, sharing some of what I had learned from Sue and her guidebook. "I'd also like to visit my good friend Sharon in London. Maybe she could join us."

I didn't have to ask twice.

# And Then There Were Three

Sharon and I met in the aftermath of the 1979 Iranian revolution. Slender and Scandinavian blonde—a typical Minnesotan—she was independent of character and full of personality. After earning her PhD in psychology from the University of Minnesota, she ended up in Iran, working for the Shah to improve literacy and numeracy schools.

When that engagement came to an abrupt end, Sharon ended up working for the same company I did, Control Data, in London. Soon she was director of Professional Services for the United Kingdom.

I was vice president in charge of all international Professional Service divisions, comprising technical consulting groups in thirty-eight countries, including Sharon's. At the time it was incredible for a worldwide organization of computer techies to have two women in such key positions, and we forged a strong partnership. We developed a global strategy to broaden the company's focus on super-computer hardware to include software and services, spending time together at conferences around the world.

Whenever Sharon came to headquarters in Minneapolis, Harold and I would invite her for dinner at our home. We had many wonderful visits, and our professional relationship evolved into a deep friendship. I remember long evenings in our garden that overlooked Lake Harriet and downtown Minneapolis, drinking the California wines that were just coming into prominence, as we talked heatedly about some passion or another.

I also remember a visit to the London office, where I was shocked by Sharon's shoes.

"You're wearing flats," I pointed out, lowering my voice, as though she might be unaware of her faux pas.

At the time, high heels were considered de rigueur for female business attire. No matter that they were horribly painful for long days at the office—and even worse for traveling.

"In England," she said, "professional women don't wear heels or sexy clothes."

It was all the excuse I needed to dump my own high heels. I attribute my continued ability to walk great distances to that muscle-saving and bunion-preventing decision.

In those days, Sharon was in a relationship with a technology executive, but they never married. She would move in and out of it for a long time before finally ending it. Eventually she ended things with Control Data, too, going on to work for a number of other companies. After a stint in Miami with Knight Ridder, she became a partner with KPMG in the Management Consulting division. When she landed a job with a communications equipment maker in the Cotswolds—someplace she had always wanted to live— she bought a converted old abbey in a village outside Cheltenham, where she still resides.

Through work Sharon eventually found her husband, Graham. Of average height and build, with a fair complexion that flushed easily and thin lips often upturned in a knowing smile, he and Sharon shared her house in the Cotswolds and an apartment on the Thames in London.

Sharon and Graham were close to Harold. She joined us when Harold and I took my mother to Croatia to visit her birthplace. After Sharon and Graham became a couple, Harold and I visited them in England. Later, all four of us met in Venice, our launchpad for hiking together in the Dolomites.

One trip Sharon and Graham could not make was to Harold's memorial, which we had at home in his beloved redwood grove. Instead, on that day they went to the site of pre-Roman ruins and an ancient burial ground near their home, where they read to each other and meditated.

When the initial mourning and shock were more than I could handle, I flew to England and walked the paths around their home, going to the burial area where they had performed their own memorial. I could be silent when I needed to, go to bed at eight if I felt like it, walk alone as far as I wanted. And I could be with them when I was in the mood for company.

It came as no surprise, then, that when I thought of walking the Thames Path, I thought of Sharon.

It took about as long to sell her on the idea as it had Linda.

# Not Quite a Plan

"Do you have any idea what the weather's like in England in the middle of winter?"

My friend Frank was convinced I had lost my mind.

"We lived in Holland for several years," he continued, his question apparently rhetorical, "and you just can't believe how cold and damp it is. England will be wetter yet! And do you know how short the days are? You're nuts to consider a trip this time of year. I haven't seen you without your down jacket in weeks, and it's balmy here compared to there!"

"Don't worry," I reassured him. "My friends and I have all lived in Minnesota—we know cold! All I care about is that we'll be alive and heading somewhere. We can always hang out in a pub if it gets too cold."

Linda, Sharon, and I had decided to walk the Thames Path in the middle of February. I had done a modest bit of preliminary research, but we had only held a few short conversations about planning. None of us had gotten into details like the ones Frank brought up.

The Thames runs through one of the most populous and modern countries in the world, ending in cosmopolitan London. I could see worrying about preparing for a trek in Kashmir, where altitude and terrorists and remoteness are concerns, but not about walking through England. We could decide each day how far to walk. Given that Sue and John had done the trail in October without hotel reservations, certainly we wouldn't have to make them very far in advance in February, when apparently no sane person would consider going! And we could take a bus or train if we got too tired, cold, or wet to walk.

Doing a little more research, I learned that the entire trail is 185 miles long. Inaugurated on July 24, 1996, it begins at the river's source in the remote Cotswolds west of London and ends in Woolrich, a town just a few miles from the sea in southeast London, within the Royal Borough of Greenwich. Since I also learned that in winter there's a high risk of flooding in the early section of the trail, I thought we should walk from Oxford to London, then on to Greenwich, where the Thames Barrier would herald the end of our walk. In total, we would do a hundred-twenty-mile stretch.

Most of those miles would follow the route of a towpath created during the industrial revolution, when rivers and canals were the main means of moving freight. The idea of turning the towpath into a walkway began with the formation in 1962 of the River Thames Society, which also aimed to extend the path west to the river's source and east through London. The idea gained momentum in 1973, when a like-minded group, the Ramblers, joined the effort.

It would take twenty-three years for the Society and the Ramblers, along with other campaigners, to bring to fruition what is now known officially as the Thames Path National Trail. In addition to negotiating with landowners and political entities, parts of the towpath that had eroded or been washed away needed to be restored. In twenty-two places, ferries that historically enabled river crossings no longer existed. Footbridges needed to be built; where they weren't, the trail would have to be diverted from the towpath and cross the river elsewhere.

In addition to flooding, I read that the prevailing winds in winter go from west to east, which made that the best direction to head, with the wind at our backs. I figured we could walk a leisurely ten miles a day.

Apart from the Cicerone book Sue brought me after mushrooming, there weren't many guides about the trail. I ordered the only other one I could find, *The Thames Path* by David Sharp. Where the Cicerone book goes from "the sea to the source," this one lets walkers "follow England's river from its peaceful source into the heart of the capital." I was relieved to find it, since I knew from experience how difficult it is to follow a guidebook in the opposite direction.

After only a few brief additional communications, we had a date, February 17, and a starting point: Oxford.

# It's Cold Out There

At the end of January a deadly cold wave brought freezing temperatures and snow to much of Europe. It was all over the news: more than 800 deaths. In early February the UK Meteorological Office issued severe weather warnings. By February 10, even more heavy snow and freezing temperatures were hitting records. The forecast was grim.

Meanwhile, our February 16 departure drew near. I knew I didn't need to feel responsible for Linda and Sharon. All the same, I was the one with the clever idea for a hundred-twenty-mile river walk in what was proving to be the coldest winter in decades. Neither of them canceled, however, so we were still on.

My packing list changed a bit. I added a few more layers, as well as my water-resistant hiking gloves. I bought us all plastic ponchos at the Dollar Store and packed some garbage bags to cover our backpacks in case of rain or snow. I got Throat Coat herbal teas and cold medicine. I made sure that my rain parka was still waterproof by wearing it in the shower, as I remembered Harold doing before he returned a twenty-year-old Gore-Tex parka that had started leaking.

As I packed in San Francisco, the sun shined, the temperature was in the sixties, and the days were growing longer. The daffodils in Golden Gate Park were in bloom, the tulip trees in full flower. Cherry blossoms lined the paths of Stow Lake. Kites flew over the Marina Green.

And suddenly it was Thursday.

Running for the door, I grabbed my father's yellow handkerchief—a memento from the town from which he fled Russia, a reminder that made me feel closer to him when I traveled—and jumped into a taxi, headed for the airport.

# A Routine Exam

It started out an ordinary day.

Doors and windows were open throughout the house, inviting inside not only the warm, pine-scented breeze but even more of the glorious sunshine that, since morning, had set the landscape aburst with color—the greens of the leaves and needles richer, the golds of the grasses on the distant hills and the poppies in the backyard unquestionably brighter, the blue of the vast, cloudless sky somehow deeper.

Looking at his watch, Harold got up from his living room chair, silenced the two Italian lovers' melodrama just as it was about to crescendo, and grabbed his wallet and keys.

After a leisurely drive down a wooded lane, through immaculate rows of vineyards, and, finally, into town, he parked the car and walked into the doctor's office. A year had passed. It was time for his routine physical.

Soon growing impatient in the small but cozy waiting room—the doctor inevitably running behind—Harold leafed through magazines without paying much attention. From the other side of the room a squirming boy with a runny nose smiled at him without a word.

Relieved when the nurse finally appeared at the door and greeted him by name, Harold followed her down a short hall. When they got to a scale, he stepped on it. He then rolled up his sleeve and held out his arm, flinching slightly as pressure enveloped it. Rolling his sleeve back down, he followed the nurse to the examination room, where he settled into a large, adjustable chair facing a human-anatomy poster. Again, he waited.

What felt like an eternity later, the doctor appeared, rushed, apologetic, friendly, and businesslike. Dressed the part, over his fit, average-size frame he wore a white lab coat. A stethoscope hung around his neck. He held a green file folder in one hand, a silver pen at the ready in the other.

"Family OK? How you been feeling? Any issues?"

The normal course of events followed. Harold answered familiar questions. He breathed deeply, and he coughed on command. When asked to drop his pants, he dutifully did as told, looking forward to getting it over, so he could get on with his day.

Momentarily distracting himself by trying to think about something other than the awkward, invasive procedure, he was snapped back to attention by the sense something was off.

"Everything OK?" he asked the doctor, who, rather than expediently performing the standard check, had paused. Without a word, he doubled down on a particular area, reapplying pressure from different angles, as though doubting what he felt—even, perhaps, hoping he hadn't felt it.

"Well, probably," the doctor tried to reassure him, his voice forced, strained as though it now belonged to someone else. "We should do some tests, though, just to be sure."

*Sure of what?* Harold thought to ask—but there was no need.

When the results came back a week later, our worst fears proved true: Harold had prostate cancer.

The good news—insofar as there was any—was that it was operable. And, at first, the surgery, which took place several weeks later, was deemed a success.

It wasn't until six months later that we got more bad news: the cancer was back—with a vengeance. Harold was given a year and a half to live.

We thought the rollercoaster ride was over. It had barely even begun.

Facing Harold's mortality head on, we let ourselves feel the shock, fear, and maddening uncertainty. We educated ourselves, learning everything we could about not only how to prolong his life but also ensure he would have the best possible quality of it for the duration.

At the same time, while it was true our world had been turned upside-down, we were determined not to take it lying down. After all, other than the cancer—which he wouldn't have even known he had, if it weren't for the check-up—Harold was healthy. He still had plenty of life in him, and we were going to make the best possible use of every last ounce of it.

And so we climbed Mount Kenya. We spent a very special month in northern Italy with a group of close family and friends in a house on Lago Maggiore. Our kids were there, along with their boyfriend and girlfriend, respectively—the ones they would end up marrying. My mother came, as did my brother and sister-in-law. Harold's sister and brother-in-law joined as well. It was an unforgettable trip that would prove one of the last times the entire family was together.

We did lots of other things, too, our best to fit every unlived life experience into that year, which the doctors insisted was Harold's last.

    Little could we have known just how wrong they were.

# Voice of an Angel

The Eastgate Hotel was full. Located in the center of Oxford, on its famous High Street, the hotel's brick-and-stone ground level supported two additional floors. They were covered in stucco and featured leaded-glass bay windows, topped by yet another story peeking out the roof through prominent dormers. As I checked in people were being turned away.

"I'm sorry, but we've called all the neighboring towns, and I cannot find you a room within twenty miles," explained the harried front-desk clerk to a couple with way too much luggage.

This was not what I had imagined when planning our low-key winter walk, one with little need for prearranged accommodations, since all the hotels were sure to be empty. It was the middle of winter! There was a deadly cold wave! Was I the only one who read the news?

The desk clerk said my room would be ready soon, adding that she could keep my bag if I wanted to have lunch. I confirmed that Sharon and Linda also had rooms, glad we had booked two nights—the second just a precaution, in case of unforeseen travel delays. Unbeknownst to us, we had arrived at an end-of-term break, which was why everything was full.

*What were we thinking?* I wondered, taking in the chaotic hotel lobby. *Our plan is to walk ten miles a day, but there aren't any hotels available for twenty miles in any direction?*

We needed an alternate plan. Instead I decided—for what was to be the first of many times over the days that followed—not to worry about that or anything else. Unaffected by jet lag, I felt great. I was ready to explore.

Given that the town was founded more than a thousand years ago, it came as no surprise that its center was like a museum of historic architecture, the houses, storefronts, schools, and churches often built in the same tawny stone also used on my hotel. Apart from the comparatively broad, relatively straight arteries converging at Carfax, site of a twelfth-century tower considered the official center of town, most of Oxford is characterized by curving lanes and hidden alleys. They weave throughout the commercial and residential areas and seemingly innumerable campuses as organically as waterways following the contours of a landscape.

In spite of the horror stories about the weather, as I stepped back outside, it didn't seem that cold. Since Oxford's two universities and their many colleges were on break, the streets were full of people. Families strolled with animated children, some laughing, some crying, others wide-eyed with curiosity. Street musicians performed, and a crowd gathered around a tightrope walker demonstrating awe-inspiring balance. I took a seat at a restaurant within sight of him, enjoying the spectacle and a leisurely lunch. Then I went wandering.

Walking down High Street (locally referred to as simply "The High"), I appreciated that the town retained its flavor of yesteryear, having resisted becoming lined with the cliché "ye olde shoppes" seen in so many tourist destinations, trite bastardizations of traditional establishments and full of cheap, disposable souvenirs more likely to be made in China than by local artisans. Instead, this was a thriving area of retail shops, restaurants, and cafés. Like my hotel, most of the buildings were three or four stories and covered in stucco. Some of their roofs, which were often punctuated by brick chimneys, were pitched, others were flat. Their large, multi-paned windows never had shutters, keeping the fronts of the buildings clean and simple.

I followed The High past a building with an ornate stone façade. Down the block, a large, even more ornate spire took to the sky. Taking a narrow side street, its gutters made of brick, sidewalks comprised of pavers, I came upon a garden and a church with a tower. Greenery tumbled over a wall as the alley veered left, revealing more walls, these with windows but no entrances. Beyond one of them, I spied elaborate pinnacles decorating a large church, like candles on a cake.

A house built over the lane followed. I passed under it, coming upon a sign welcoming me to New College—ironically posted on a barrier in front of a closed door. Today the name, too, seems ironic, given that the school was founded in 1379. The University of Oxford, of which New College is just one of thirty-nine colleges, is even older. In fact, it's the second oldest university in the world. Only Italy's University of Bologna, where teaching began around 1088, has been in continuous operation longer.

What came next caught me off guard. I recognized it, but I hadn't expected to come across it now: the Bridge of Sighs. Officially called Hertford Bridge, the elegant structure connects two of Hertford College's buildings. It became known as the Bridge of Sighs because of its supposed resemblance to Venice's famed bridge of the same name.

Other than the fact that they both joined two buildings, as I looked at Hertford Bridge now, I didn't see many similarities. The Venetian original is crafted in white limestone and built over a canal. Its two windows on each side are covered in stonework like lattice, reminiscent of the Arab *mashrabiyas* that allow for viewing from inside without being observed from the outside. In comparison, Hertford Bridge is built of tawny stone and features no fewer than nine tall, clear windows on both sides. Anyone traversing the bridge must make a slight ascent followed by a corresponding descent. I was more reminded of the vaulted Rialto Bridge than the level Bridge of Sighs. Still, regardless of how much it did or not actually resemble its Venetian namesake, it was a harmonious, visually pleasing structure.

I now found myself on a main road, before me a wrought-iron gate opening onto a square that likely pertained to another college. Continuing past a pub, I turned onto a narrow, mostly residential lane. Further down it, a lone tree bore the only visible testimony to the natural world. Why were trees so few and far between on Oxford's streets?

Walking around a metal gate keeping out traffic, I was buffeted by the rush of a busy two-lane thoroughfare. I followed yet another wall—this one topped with a parapet—and soon found myself back where I started: on The High, my hotel on the opposite corner.

Looking both ways as I crossed the street, I was reminded that I needed to confirm details for Evensong, a renowned Friday night choral service at Magdalen College. On their own walk, Sue and John had heard such good things about Evensong that they had cut short their trip to attend. They weren't disappointed.

"I will never forget the angelic voices of those young

male sopranos," Sue had recalled when she dropped off the guidebook, as though transported back to the performance.

It was meant to be. We were not only starting our trek in Oxford, but by coincidence we had arrived on a Friday.

Returning to the hotel, I found that Sharon, Graham, and Linda had checked in. After calling them down to the lobby, short introductions took place, and we turned our attention to sorting out Evensong plans. Even though the Eastgate was a short distance from Magdalen College, figuring out the exact time and location of the performance proved more complicated than I'd been led to believe. I asked the front-desk clerk for more information.

"Actually," he explained, his stout body threatening to burst open the tight button-down under his vest, "Evensong takes place every night, and not only at Maudlin but in several chapels around town." He had silver hair and wore thick glasses that he took on and off, depending on whether he was looking at the computer screen.

"My friends said that Magdalen is the best," I told him again, looking for validation.

"I don't know if it's the best, but I have heard Maudlin is a very good one," he allowed.

I paused, glancing at my friends, wondering if they were confused like I was.

"And what about Magdalen?" I asked, trying again.

"Oh, of course," he laughed. "I'm so sorry! We pronounce it *Maudlin* here—I figured you were just saying it your way, and I was saying it ours!"

I looked at my friends again, all of us bursting into laughter. I had no idea how the locals had turned the pronunciation of *Magdalen* into *Maudlin*, but as the visitor, I didn't get much say in the matter. What I would say going forward, however, was *Maudlin*.

It wasn't until later that I learned the mix-up wasn't merely a question of differing accents. When, in 1458, the founder of the college included a statute for a choir, he made specific reference to how the name should be pronounced. "Magdalene" was to be pronounced "Maudlin," because in late medieval English Mary Magdalene was "Maudelen," derived from the Old French "Madelaine."

Our new friend went on to share that, due to the term break, tonight the Magdalen choir was incomplete: only adult men would be singing—not the young boys whose voices had so enraptured Sue.

Seeing our disappointed faces, the clerk made a few calls. It turned out that New College would have their full mixed-age choir.

"I know exactly where it is," I said, recalling my earlier stroll.

The Vienna Boys Choir's "Ave Maria" echoing in my head, we went up to our rooms to put on warm clothes.

As we stepped outside shortly after and headed for the 6:15 service, I was relieved to see that my friends seemed to be taking to each other. I hadn't even realized I'd been holding my breath, questioning the wisdom of diving into days together with two women who had never met. So many people have horror stories about traveling with someone they thought they knew well, but who turned out to be a totally incompatible travel companion.

Despite the relatively early hour, it was already getting dark as we walked through Oxford. I was reminded of just how short winter days were this far north.

We found New College readily enough but wandered aimlessly, unable to find the chapel. When a donnish older gentleman named Giles offered to show us the way, I hesitated. We needed to find the chapel, but I feared this conservatively dressed, proper English gentleman was a little too tightly wound to make for a pleasant guide. I was wrong. Giles proved so warm-hearted and eager to help that I had to concede that even someone who initially seemed so stuffy could be good company. From here on out I would be less quick to judge, more open to talking with strangers.

Though technically a chapel, the structure we entered was more like a tall, narrow cathedral. Elaborate carvings covered the walls, and a small number of chairs and pews lined both sides of a center aisle, facing each other rather than the front of the church. About a quarter of the seats was filled by a small choir. We were about to partake of a very intimate performance.

Giles was of the opinion that New College's choir had the best voices in Oxford, with All Souls and Magdalen close seconds. We were in no position to compare, but he couldn't have been far off.

The choir was amazing, bolstered by the impeccable acoustics of the chapel, evidently designed not only to exalt God but the voices of those singing his praises. Even as the rest of the ensemble sang, their voices blending into an almost impeccably unified whole, one particular boy somehow stood out, his voice crystalline. I found myself disconsolate reflecting how age would inevitably steal his particular gift.

And then I found myself shedding tears.

I hadn't seen them coming. One moment I was listening to the choir, drawn to the young boy's singular voice. But when, in the next, he broke away from the group and launched into a solo, it was as if an angel swooped down from the altar and carried me away on his wings. The perfect pitch of his divine falsetto, the purity and innocence, resonated with my very being, unlocking something deep in my core. As I caught my breath, emotion unexpectedly surged forth, tears cascading down my cheeks.

As they did, I felt the ice lining my heart begin to melt. Since Harold's death it had protected me from being overwhelmed by "too much" emotion, cutting me off from my normally easy tears. Now, an ineffable power in a young boy's voice helped them to flow again, a preliminary but important step forward in my healing.

Moved by still more tears, now ones of gratitude, I could hardly think of a better way to inaugurate our trip.

---

My friends no longer strangers, all of us bonded by the performance, we walked back to the Eastgate. We decided to skip a big dinner in favor of the lobby bar, a well-lit space of polished wood floors and exposed-brick walls. Its immaculate shelves of liquor, beers on tap, and comfortable bar stools were exactly what we needed.

Since he was leaving in the morning, Graham offered to buy us a drink to send us on our way. I had just spent time in Cuba, where I had gotten hooked on mojitos. My expectations low but figuring it was worth a shot, I asked the bartender if there was any chance he could make my new favorite drink. He vanished into the breakfast room, only to return with fresh mint.

Although we had no way of knowing it at the time, every village pub and inn, no matter how small, would prove to have fresh mint and some sort of rum—and we weren't about to miss an opportunity to enjoy it. The first tradition of our trip was born.

"How far are you planning to walk tomorrow?" asked Graham, the scent of mint perfuming the air.

Linda, Sharon, and I looked at each other. We hadn't even discussed when we were starting, let alone any other logistics. Sharon and Linda had bought David Sharp's *The Thames Path* but hadn't taken the time to read it. I had paged through it but quickly got bored.

"And how will you get your things from hotel to hotel?" he continued, oblivious to our cluelessness.

"Maybe we don't need to carry much," I said, it suddenly occurring to me that we needed almost nothing on this trip. It was nowhere near the polar cold I had expected, and people were dressed respectably but casually. We wouldn't be playing much dress-up.

I decided to leave everything with Graham, except for a change of underwear, a second top, some socks, and my wash kit. He could take the rest with him to London. Like when Sharon and I had trekked in the Dolomites a couple of years earlier, we could treat this expedition as a number of overnight trips, rinsing out our clothes in the sink, as needed.

Linda and I were totally wiped out. Jet lag, the walking, and the drinks had done us in. The group decided to meet for breakfast at 8:30 and finalize any outstanding details—which was to say, just about all of them.

I arrived at breakfast with a very light pack, since most of what I was taking was already on my back. I was thrilled to have eliminated the need to ferry luggage between hotels.

No sooner did I see the bags Sharon and Linda were carrying, however, than I realized I had neglected to clue them in. Once I explained my thinking that less was more, worried they might not buy into the idea, they jumped at it. Since we were all in this together—none of us would have clean clothes to change into—the decision was easy. We would present a united front when dealing with any potential pushback at hotels and restaurants. It was a liberating moment, and I was relieved things were clicking into place, feeling blessed that both friends were so easygoing.

Agreeing on the day's journey was easy, too. We would head for a town about ten miles downriver called Abingdon, which was on a bus line. That was key, since the lack of hotel rooms meant we would have to return to Oxford for the night.

We finished breakfast and went upstairs to pack our bags, so Graham could take them to London. I felt a tinge of regret that he wasn't joining us. But we all understood this was a trip for three women.

A half hour later we were off.

During a previous marriage, Graham had lived on a segment of the trail. All the same, he had never walked it. He was born and raised in England, and he and Sharon now had homes on both ends of the path. No matter. Even though they loved to walk the countryside, outside of London the trail remained a mystery to them both.

Graham worried we would be walking in towns and on busy roads much of the time, which was his limited experience of the Thames. And it made sense: the trail traversed one of the most populated areas of the world. We would never be more than twenty miles from a city, not much more than a hundred miles from London.

As we pulled up to the bridge where our adventure would commence, we saw a path heading downriver. An arching sign held aloft by two lampposts proclaimed: "Head of the River." Although it turned out to be the entryway for a hotel of the same name, it felt an appropriate starting point for our trip.

Sharon asked Graham to take a picture of the three of us in front of the sign. The photo shows us grinning broadly, dressed for the elements, and holding our backpacks, ready to go.

There is no picture by me to commemorate the trip—I didn't bring my camera. For a dedicated photographer, leaving it behind was an even bigger decision than what clothes to take. In fact, without my camera I felt naked in a different sort of way. What would I look through if not my viewfinder? What would I see if I wasn't composing? What about the beautiful images I might miss?

Graham jumped back into his car. We waved him off and started walking, hoping we were on the right side of the river.

# Bridges

We weren't.

A few minutes walking, and something didn't feel right. It was beautiful at the riverside, but the trail wasn't following the water very closely—and we vaguely remembered needing to cross at some point. Since our most important guiding principal was to stay on the same side of the river as the trail, our uncertainty was not a good sign.

We stopped and got out the guidebook. Sure enough, we needed to be on the opposite bank. We should have crossed the first bridge, which, appropriately enough—considering our lackadaisical attitude toward planning—turned out to be called Folly Bridge.

Bridges have played an important role in my life: bridges between worlds old and new; bridges surrounding my home in San Francisco; a bridge where I fell in love. Even bridges that have been bombed.

Presently I was trying to bridge two worlds, the one where I'd lived for the past thirty-five years, centered around my relationship with Harold, and the one that followed, from which he would be physically absent. To the extent I had no choice, I had moved nominally into that new world. Closer to the truth was that I was frozen between the two.

Unwilling to let go of the world I had lost, I held at bay the pain that might come with exploring the one taking its place. I avoided large gatherings, extended conversations with old friends, and talking about my feelings.

Walking was a perfect example of my increasing isolation. Here on the trail, I had chosen to walk with two friends. At home, I'd stopped walking with anyone.

For years, Harold and I had done our regularly scheduled morning stroll with a group of friends. Once he was gone, I started avoiding it—and them. At first I just skipped the coffee afterward. Then I started emailing—not calling—that I wouldn't be able to make it, neither for the walk nor the coffee. I didn't stop walking, though. Now I just did it on my own.

Perhaps if I hadn't begun spending so much time alone, I would have heeded the advice friends had given me repeatedly about not making any big changes in the aftermath of Harold's death. They were right, after all: I was in no mental state to make major life decisions.

But I was alone that day mere weeks later, when I not only happened to find myself in the City but driving by a building I knew all too well.

In the late 1980s Harold and I made a major life decision of our own. We were happily living in Minnesota, where we had met and married. I was between jobs.

"Do you think we'll always want to be in Minnesota?" he asked one day, as I bemoaned the lack of local startup opportunities.

"Until the job that brought me here, I'd never considered a month in Minnesota, never mind a lifetime!" I exclaimed. "Who would have thought I could be this happy here? But what about you?"

"I don't want to stay in my job forever, and I can't imagine spending the rest of my life here. I don't want to be this cold when I get old!" he laughed.

The kids were graduating high school and would soon be leaving Minnesota for college. My mother was alone in San Francisco. Nearby Silicon Valley was arguably the best place in the world for opportunities in high tech. Harold had no interest in returning to his native New Jersey.

I got a job in Berkeley. Harold would commute for a year, before giving up his own job and joining me. Near Ghirardelli Square in San Francisco I found a condo to rent while we transitioned. The landlord, Gordon, was a wonderful man regularly traveling back and forth between the US and Germany, where his mother-in-law was ill. When I first saw his condo, he told me I could hold onto any existing furniture. I kept only a small dining table and the chandelier over it. I didn't want anything intruding on the astonishing floor-to-ceiling views of the San Francisco Bay.

Harold and I got a good price for our beautiful home on Lake Harriet, a prime piece of Minneapolis real estate. We were elated, until we realized the revenue would barely make a dent in the purchase of even a modest house in San Francisco, where teardowns were running more than a million dollars.

Our inexpensive rental with breathtaking views suddenly became a much more attractive, longer-term solution. We ended up staying for nine years. All that time, Gordon was a gem. He never raised the rent, and whenever he was in town he stopped by for tea.

We were in the condo during the 1989 earthquake, which severely damaged the neighboring Marina District. Since our building was built on bedrock, it suffered only minor damage. Other than the chandelier falling onto the table, leaving a big scratch, our apartment made it through the disaster unscathed.

When Harold and I stopped working after he was diagnosed with cancer, we started spending more time in Healdsburg, where we had bought our weekend house overlooking the redwood forests of the Russian River Valley. My mother was getting older and had a large home in the City. We gave up the condo, moved some stuff into my childhood bedroom, and made that our pied-à-terre.

As the memories flashed through my mind, I turned the car around, parked, and went inside the building.

"Do you have any units for sale?" I asked the concierge, an attractive young Latino with a well-groomed beard that matched his dark vest.

"I think there's one available on the fifth floor," he replied.

"Is there someone who can show it to me?"

"Sure. Do you have an agent? They can set something—"

"No, I mean *now*. Is there someone who can show me the unit now?"

"Oh," he hesitated, caught off guard by the unexpected urgency and taking a moment to consider his response. "Actually, Liliana is an agent, and she lives in the building."

"Is Liliana free?"

An hour later I owned the condo.

The outside world had always seen me as an extrovert. Now,

in the aftermath of Harold's passing, I was surprised to recognize myself in a definition that challenged my notion of what it meant to be an introvert: *an introvert expends energy when with people and needs time alone to recharge.* That is me. I enjoy intense interaction with others, but I need to be on my own to reenergize.

My self-imposed isolation, taken to a new level by the impulse buy of my place in the City, could have been seen by others as a period of soul-searching to start rebuilding. In truth I was hiding, as much from people as I was from my feelings. Or lack thereof.

I was numb. I felt empty.

I continued to have at my disposal a persona I had embodied for many years. It took little effort to maintain it. I traveled. I photographed. Although on the inside I still felt blank and hollow, on the outside I appeared to be living again. In fact, the outside world seemed to think I had my act together, that I was dealing with Harold's death "amazingly." Closer to the truth was that I was putting up an amazing front.

"It's not easy," I had confessed when a close friend asked how I was feeling. What I really wanted to say was that it was agonizing.

"I know what you mean," my friend offered. "I recently lost my mother."

My chest tightened and my jaw clenched. I practically snapped back, *no, you don't know what I mean—you don't have any idea.*

I, too, had lost my parents. I loved them, and their deaths were very painful. I still think of both Papa and Mama often. All the same, assuming our parents don't die when we're young, we know that someday we'll lose them.

By the time we do, we've grown up. We've made our own lives; we've emancipated ourselves. If we have a partner, we share our days and nights with them—not with our parents. We share with them an intimacy altogether different from the bond between parent and child. And so, as painful as it was to lose a parent, for me it scarcely compared to losing my soulmate.

"Yes," my friend insisted, "but clearly Harold's death is not bothering you as much as my losing my mother did."

My blood began to boil. Who was she to tell me the depth of my feeling? How dare she compare our pain, as though she were trying to outdo me? She had no clue. I longed to tell her how hard it was, to give her a glimpse of my unvoiced agony, the debilitating sense of loss I had to deal with every single day. There was no point. She wasn't going to get it.

I changed the subject, reeling from the unexpected insight into how well I was hiding my pain. I had also learned a difficult lesson. If one of my closest friends was unable to make space for my sorrow—even felt the need to one-up mine—with whom could I share it? The only person who came close was my brother. He understood—he, too, had lost Harold, after all—but we didn't talk about it. Better to keep it to myself, to deal with it on my own terms.

Meanwhile, my grief kept me from envisioning other ways to live than what I had known, ways that could be mine, were I to explore them. For now I couldn't see—let alone cross—the bridge that might get me there.

And so perhaps it should have come as no surprise that here on the Thames Path National Trail we missed Folly Bridge the first time around. Now though, having backtracked almost all the way to where we started, there it was again: three elegant stone arches connecting one side of the deep green water with the other.

    We crossed the bridge.

# Three's Company

Boats raced up and down the river, oars slipping into the water with scarcely a ripple, resurfacing a moment later with barely a splash.

Now that we had made it over to the correct side of the river, we had no trouble finding our way. Children and dogs played along the path, this section wet from recent rains. Coaches bicycled past us, shouting encouragement and imprecations to their teams on the water. The lawns that bordered the trail were a lush green, but the weather was cold and gray. We barely noticed. Our inaugural-day enthusiasm pushed us along, and we made good progress, passing a few boat houses as we followed tree-lined banks alternating with open fields, the terrain mostly flat.

A little over an hour into our stroll, we came upon a major lock. Like others we'd see along the way, this canal-like enclosure had gates at each end and was used to raise or lower boats along sections of the river where dams caused the water levels to vary. In all, there are forty-five locks on the non-tidal River Thames, the first of which appeared all the way back in the 1630s.

I fell behind Sharon and Linda, who understood and respected my need for space. Meanwhile, they got to know each other, pleased to discover they had an amazing amount in common. They had both grown up in the Midwest, and they had even got PhDs in the same subject—psychology— at the very same school, the University of Minnesota, graduating just a few years apart.

It was no coincidence that I'd invited two friends, as opposed to one. I knew that periodically I would need alone time. I've always been that way. There would be intervals—like now—when I didn't feel like talking, moments when, without giving it much, if any, thought, I would lag behind or go up ahead. When I did, Sharon and Linda could talk to each other. Again I was relieved they were hitting it off.

Beneath the excitement I displayed outwardly about the trip, I was aware of a persistent undercurrent of melancholy. But I didn't grieve. The horrid experience at my computer had felt too close to self-pity, to self-indulgence in sorrow. And so I said I would never grieve again—and I didn't.

What I was feeling was different. I wasn't dwelling on the injustice of it all, looking for reasons, asking why me. I was simply feeling the hollow ache of an absence, the loss of something very deep and important that, from one moment to the next, was no longer there. I felt a relentless disquiet throughout my body, an agonizing yearning in my heart, a hole ripped open inside me. Until it was filled, I wouldn't be myself.

As we passed under a railroad bridge, the dark brick of its foundation besmirched with white paint that looked thrown at it haphazardly, as well as yellow splotches of what appeared to be lichens, I once again fell into Sharon and Linda's orbit. As I did, I caught random snippets of their conversation, catching up on things I didn't know much about or had simply forgotten. Sharon learned about the businesses Linda had run.

Before we realized it, four hours had passed. Mother Nature, however, was about to bring us back to the moment.

"Was that a raindrop?" Sharon asked.

We all looked up to the sky, as though, if in fact it were starting to rain, merely feeling it wouldn't be enough; as though we'd need to see it to believe it.

"The sky has gotten a lot darker," Linda observed.

Tree branches stirred anxiously, as though trying to get our attention. Ripples agitated the river surface. The air smelled of ozone.

"I felt one!" I exclaimed, as a big drop landed on my face.

It was followed by another. And another.

"Oh god," Sharon cried out, as the wind whipped up, "it's about to pour!"

And it did, catching us unawares with no place to hide.

Fifteen minutes later, soaked but laughing, we reached another lock; specifically, Abingdon Lock. Water suddenly on both sides of us, we followed a dirt trail and ascended a narrow metal walkway. To our left, the river surface was almost perfectly smooth, punctuated only by scattered raindrops, now thankfully greatly reduced in number, the downpour having moved on. To our right, roaring cascades plummeted into what, on first look, might have seemed a different body of water, given that it was several feet lower than what we saw to our left. In reality, of course, it was the same river.

Midway across the walkway we came to a wall of steel girders topped with a wooden roof. Over the girders, large chains wound around metal pipes like thread on a spool. The water level was controlled by releasing and recoiling the chains, which raised and lowered doors hidden below the water surface—or at least out of sight from our vantage point above them. The entire structure was an engineering marvel, and—since we were already soaked—we paused to admire it.

Ten minutes later we came upon another marvel: Abingdon Bridge, which heralded our arrival at our destination, the small town of Abingdon itself. Our plan was to have a late lunch, then catch a bus back to Oxford.

On our way into town, we passed a corner where a rambunctious group of young men wearing athletic wear and carrying duffle bags whooped it up. When we interrupted to ask them where to eat, they enthusiastically recommended King's Head and Bell, a pub from the 1600s.

"Uh oh," said Sharon as we entered shortly after. She looked as though she'd just taken a shower in her clothes, or perhaps been pulled out of the river after being swept away by it.

"Are we sure we want to do this?" laughed Linda, looking down at our mud-clumped shoes and the sloppy pools forming around them, drop by drop.

After our long walk, the stone-baked pizzas and fresh coffee promised on the building façade could hardly have been more enticing. Now that we were inside, however, we weren't sure we belonged here. The rock walls were painted an immaculate white, part of the dining room was carpeted in light gray, and, unlike the stone floor near the bar or the old wood beams overhead, the tables and chairs looked as though they might be new.

"We're a muddy mess!" I agreed, wondering if we should head back outside. The irresistible aromas wafting out of the kitchen held me in place.

"Table for three?" asked a young blonde woman, a smile on her face, as though she hadn't even noticed our damp backpacks and jackets. Scarcely missing a beat, she grabbed three menus from a podium and turned to show us to our table.

It was a scene that would repeat itself over the course of our walk: no matter how sweaty, wet, or dirty we were, no matter how informal or fancy the establishment, nobody cared how we looked.

The friendly hostess seated us at a table near a gas fireplace radiating welcome heat, returning immediately with the water we so badly craved. When the food arrived a short while later, it exceeded our expectations. Battered pickles started us off, followed by a mushroom, spinach, and truffle oil pizza for me, a pulled pork bun for Sharon, and a buttermilk chicken sandwich that Linda would talk about for days. To top it all off, we couldn't resist sharing the "Cheesecake Fixes Everything" dessert, which it did—with a little help from the ice cream alongside it.

Finding the bus back to Oxford was easy. The trip took less than half an hour and, after some time to regroup in our rooms, we headed back out for afternoon tea at the oldest coffee shop in England.

Aptly named The Grand Café, as we walked inside, greeted by a familiar rich aroma, the interior's high ceiling, marble columns topped with elegant iconic capitals, and mosaic-covered bar made quite an impression. After taking a seat at one of the much less grandiose wooden tables, we ordered afternoon tea. It, too, failed to disappoint: finger sandwiches and smoked salmon; cream cheese and cucumber, egg mayonnaise and cress; two kinds of scones, and lemon and chocolate desserts. Clearly we had come to the right place!

But was it really the oldest coffee shop in England?

Looking around, to me the place looked well-loved but not necessarily hundreds of years old. After admiring the candleholders in the shape of arms sticking out of the walls, my eyes fell upon a menu the server had left behind.

*According to Samuel Pepys' Diary, 1650, The Grand Café is the site of the first coffee house in England, and now an Oxford institution.*

Needing to know more, on the café's website I learned that, over the course of its history, in addition to serving as the coffee house established in 1650 by a Jewish entrepreneur named Jacob, the building had also been "an Inn, an Hotel, a Grocer's Shop, a Co-op and a Post Office." Its current incarnation as The Grand Café dated to a surprisingly recent 1997.

So where was the actual oldest café in England?

Right across the street.

Queen's Lane Coffee House was apparently founded in 1654 by another Jewish entrepreneur, Cirques Jacobus. Although it had obviously moved locations since then—we were on the The High, after all, not Queen's Lane—the establishment still laid claim to being the oldest café in England. Thankfully, on its website it addressed the confusion.

The Grand Café, it explained, is the site of England's first coffee house. However, as I had already learned, it has been many other things since its inception. In contrast, Queen's Lane, which opened in 1654, has been a coffee house ever since. So, whereas The Grand Café opened first, Queen's Lane has served as an actual café for longer—longer, it was claimed, than any other café in Europe.

The explanation on Queen's Lane's website ended with a diplomatic, "Both of us are proud to be cafés with historical value."

I was glad to see there was room for both cafés to be the "oldest," each in their own way.

Putting down my phone and inhaling the rich aroma of my Earl Gray, the cup warm in my hands, with a knowing smile I said to Linda and Sharon, "I guess I don't need to ask what you want to do tonight."

"Evensong!" they chimed, as though on cue.

We knew that the full choir was singing at Magdalen that night, and we couldn't wait to hear how they compared to the one at New College. Had time allowed, we would have loved to stay one more night and attend Evensong at All Souls, too. But we had already stayed in Oxford longer than planned, and we had a trail to walk!

That night we made the short stroll to the Magdalen chapel, which was similar to New College's, albeit a little less ornate. Linda and Sharon preferred this choir to New College's, but I missed that singular young voice that had touched me so deeply. All the same, both choirs are world famous—Magdalen's even won a Gramophone Award—and it was hard to find fault with either.

As the last note echoed off the stone interior of the chapel, my heart full and my spirit lifted, once again I was reminded of the healing power of music. I couldn't help but think how much Harold, my great opera lover, would have enjoyed it.

And then I saw us together in another church full of music, at an event he had in fact very much enjoyed many years before.

# Russian Easter

I didn't realize how unusual my background was until I had to explain Russian Easter to Harold. Why was it on a different day than American Easter? Why was it the most important celebration of our year, more important even than Christmas? In the days before Google and Wikipedia, explaining was no easy task.

The questions began when I asked Harold to come to San Francisco to meet my family. While there, we would attend Russian Easter celebrations.

"Wow," Harold marveled, as we approached the Russian Orthodox cathedral on Geary Street, "I feel like we took a wrong turn and ended up in Moscow."

The Holy Virgin Cathedral, also known as the Joy of All Who Sorrow—a name that to me has always seemed more than a little ironic—is the largest of the six Russian Orthodox cathedrals outside Russia. To Harold's point, the building's architecture leaves no doubt as to its origins. Five onion domes crown the towering edifice, each covered in twenty-four-carat gold leaf and topped with a cross. More mosaics adorn the building's façade, the top half featuring six long, narrow renderings of holy men. Over the church entrance, a seventh depicts the Virgin Mary surrounded by angels.

As Harold was about to find out, the interior of the cathedral is no less impressive. We stepped inside, his eyes darting from icons to religious paintings to more mosaics. Overhead, a large chandelier illuminated the ornate space with a subdued glow.

The cathedral had filled up early with the faithful. The marginally faithful—those who, like us, went to church only on Easter and Christmas—arrived around 11:30. We looked forward to the service, but had no desire to stand from nine o'clock to two in the morning, the length of the full, seemingly interminable service. Unlike in most of my non-Russian friends' churches, in ours there is no sitting.

My brother, Alex, had got candles for everyone. At midnight the entire congregation would take to the street, filling it with candlelight. The reason for heading outside was to allow Christ to arise in privacy. Until the church emptied, he waited patiently in an elaborate casket in front of the main altar. To ensure no one woke him early, an honor guard of soldiers and scouts protected the casket, a role I had once performed.

When the time came, a procession began leaving the church, led by a small man with a big presence and long white beard. Dressed in flowing gold robes, he wore an elaborate jeweled miter on his head, carried a gold prayer book in one hand, and swung an incense lamp from the other. All the while, his deep bass voice intoned a sacred chant.

The rest of the procession followed, carrying icons and banners and swinging more incense. Wizened old believers who had spent their lives frequenting the cathedral, like the old family friends of my childhood, cradled objects of devotion in their hands. The choir brought up the rear, including my cousin Lena and her husband Vitja.

As the procession finished its circumnavigation of the church, the archbishop stood before the front doors, which had been closed.

"*Hristos voskrese!*" ("Christ has risen!"), he proclaimed.

"*Vo istinu voskrese!*" ("Indeed he has risen!"), we called back.

The choir outside was joined by one inside, their joyous, melodic voices projected over loudspeakers. The whole city must have heard the music, one of the most beautiful pieces I know, the hymn in celebration of Christ's rebirth, "*Hristos voskrese iz mertvih*" ("Christ rises from the dead"). No matter that I couldn't understand the words, since it was sung not in Russian but in the old Church Slavonic still used in the Orthodox service. The hymn was sung again and again, the archbishop repeating his blessing during the pauses. Eventually, he triumphantly reentered the cathedral, which was now empty of the casket but filled with the Holy Spirit.

What came next was the greeting with three kisses. Starting on Easter and continuing for forty days, until Ascension—the day Christ is believed to have ascended to heaven—members of the community greet each other with three pecks on the cheek. It's a ritual beloved by teenage boys, but of which young women are less fond.

The service continued inside, but we stayed outdoors, where we found ourselves surrounded by family and friends. My uncle Shura emerged from the crowd and looked Harold up and down. At 6'2" this family patriarch, the oldest of my father's brothers, had always been the tallest and most important man in the room. I was astonished as he looked up at Harold—who stood four inches taller—broke into an enormous grin, gave him a bear hug, and kissed him the traditional three times.

After the ceremony concluded, we headed home. The

table was already set for the stream of people that would wander in at all hours from churches all over the city, including many of my childhood friends. They got a kick out of toasting Harold with the vodka shots that had to be downed—*bottoms up!*—every time someone proposed a new toast.

The partying continued until four in the morning, wrapping up only so the revelers could get some rest before still more celebrations the next day.

On Easter Sunday the women stay home, filling tables with all sorts of traditional treats: Easter eggs; *kulich*, the Easter cake; *pasha*, a sweet cheese pyramid; *zakuski*, an assortment of cold hors d'oeuvres, entrées, and snacks; and an endless flow of vodka. The men travel from house to house, eating and drinking and getting progressively more rambunctious over the course of the day.

Harold stayed with me, soaking in the stories that friends and family were more than happy to share when prompted by his questions. And while the air was festive, the stories often were not. We heard tales of war and displacement, of families torn apart, of lives spent in a kaleidoscope of places: Russia, Ukraine, the Don, Siberia, Gallipoli, Shanghai, Harbin, Japan, Serbia, Berlin, Trieste, Paris, Argentina, Venezuela, Australia, and more. We heard countless others, including Tolya and Yana's.

Close friends of my family, she was the prima ballerina of the Belgrade ballet; he was its ballet master, responsible for ensuring dancers in the company maintained their skills and could perform at their best.

When Stalin and Tito had their falling out, Tolya and Yana were forced to give up their careers and the privileged lives afforded by their success. Simply because they were

Russian. With little choice but to emigrate, they moved first to Germany, before eventually settling in San Francisco, where they taught ballet. While ostensibly still part of a world they loved, it was a far cry from their glory days as stars of the Yugoslav ballet.

Then there was my childhood best friend, Alec, whose mother was a pianist of great renown. The refugee camp head was so impressed with her talent that she performed at his private events. Consequently, Alec and his family's internment in the camp was easier and shorter than most, including my family's. After less than a year, they were able to leave for a new life in South America.

What at first seemed a happy ending, however, instead proved the beginning of more unimaginable hardship.

Alec and his father were eventually granted permission to immigrate to the United States. His mother was not, a cruel twist of fate that tore apart their family. My own Mama felt so sorry for Alec that she treated him like a second son, showering him with love and affection and including him in our family vacations and celebrations.

That night Harold also heard the story of my Uncle Kolya and Aunt Lyolya. Like us, they lived in the refugee camp, San Sabba, in what is now northeastern Italy. An abandoned rice factory, I would later learn it had also served as a German concentration camp.

A mere child who didn't know better, who made friends and entertained herself with her imagination, I enjoyed life there. A grown woman accustomed to living in the comfort of her own home, Aunt Lyolya found it intolerable. Looking back, it's easy to understand why.

Whereas families like mine lived in slightly better conditions in the barracks, Kolya and Lyolya shared a single giant room with about a hundred other adults. Makeshift curtains were hung to offer a similitude of privacy, but there were no beds: they slept on cold, hard floors. Bathrooms, too, were shared and located a long walk away down dark, dusty halls. In another drab common area, we all ate bland food that varied little from day to day.

Perhaps the final blow for my aunt—a characteristic of life at San Sabba that made it feel even less distinguishable from prison—was the need for permission to the leave the premises. Even when we got it, our hours outside the factory walls were restricted.

My aunt was not only uncomfortable but bored out of her mind. So much so that even working as an indentured servant seemed better than another day at San Sabba.

Indentured servitude—becoming indebted to an employer until your debt is paid off—was still legal in 1950s Canada. Initially, though, Uncle Kolya and Aunt Lyolya weren't planning on going to Canada—their hopes were pinned on Australia. That changed from one moment to the next when a friend walked by the Australia visa-application line and told them Canada was accepting immigrants. Not wanting to test their luck, Kolya and Lyolya made the spur-of-the-moment decision to go for the safer bet. They stepped out of the Australia line and into the Canada one.

When they got to the front, they learned their friend was right: not only would they be welcomed in Canada, but they could work to repay the cost of their trip there. They accepted the arrangement.

Not long after, Lyolya and Kolya set sail on an army ship bound for Canada, landing at Halifax. From there they took a train to Toronto, where they were presented with multiple employment options: farm labor, railroad construction, hospital work. They accepted a contract as servants in a home on the west side of Toronto.

I was too young to learn all the details, let alone understand them. But I got the most important part: Uncle Kolya and Aunt Lyolya's new life in Canada was a disaster. They were treated like enslaved people. They made next to no money, had no benefits, and were charged so much for their food that their debt only grew—becoming impossible for them to repay.

The way I remember it, things got so bad that six months into the engagement Kolya and Lyolya saw no choice but to flee. After making a clandestine escape to Toronto, they lived underground until someone helped them find hospital work, Lyolya at a downtown location, Koyla at a nearby mental-health facility.

Despite being an unskilled position where he used none of his engineering expertise, Uncle Kolya actually liked his job as a night watchman, since it was there that he took up a new favorite hobby: embroidery. He loved it so much, he could do it all night. My cousin still has some of his work lovingly displayed in her home.

Hearing these stories was good for both Harold and me, albeit for different reasons. For him, they marked the beginning of years of fascination with a culture and history about which initially he knew little. For me, it led to a new way to see what seemed like nothing more than cause for embarrassment when I was a child, when I desired nothing more than to be a "real" American.

Harold always helped me see my heritage differently, to value the depth of those connections to a lost past.

# Food and Drink

After a light final breakfast, the next morning Sharon, Linda, and I grabbed our packs, said goodbye to the Eastgate, and caught the bus to Abingdon, where we had finished our hike the previous afternoon.

Our plan for the day was to walk to the tiny village of Dorchester, about eight miles downriver. Lesson learned, we had already booked a room at the White Hart Hotel, ranked number one (of two) hotels there.

Just after nine o'clock we were back on the trail. Traffic and crowds quickly a thing of the past, we found ourselves walking through bucolic countryside. Trees lined the river. Narrow lanes headed away from it. On both sides, fields extended into the distance. Mud again clung to our shoes, and water splashed our pants. It wasn't long before we looked as if we had spent the morning feeding angry pigs.

Ten o'clock came and went, and we hadn't passed anywhere that served food or coffee. Linda's feet had gotten sore by the end of the previous day, and she needed someplace to take off her shoes and put on protective tape.

"I'm sure we'll pass something soon," I said.

In truth, I wasn't sure at all.

Eventually we came to Clifton Lock. Completed in 1822, it's located south of the village of Clifton Hampden and north of Long Wittenham. Tables were set up outside the keeper's house, a handsome two-story brick dwelling with a steeply pitched roof and two chimneys. It looked like the perfect place to sit and enjoy the river, as we took a tea or coffee break. We could almost smell the scones baking behind the frilly curtains in the little kitchen's windows.

Except the place was deserted.

Like all the others we would pass. We wouldn't learn until later that the lock operators were on their winter breaks.

"They're busy all summer," the area lock manager explained, an affable, middle-aged man with a thick mustache. We happened upon him performing maintenance checks. "These paths are full of walkers then. On weekends you hardly have a moment to breathe between the visitors looking for food and drink and the boaters impatient to get down the river. This is the only time the operators can get away. It's too cold for walkers, there aren't really pleasure boats this time of year, and the commercial barges mostly don't come up this far."

Looking at our dirty clothes and wet feet, he couldn't help but ask, "So what brings you here in the middle of winter?"

We were to hear versions of this question all along the trail. We did run into a few day hikers on weekends, joggers near towns sometimes, and families out for a stroll occasionally. But no "through hikers," as those who did extended, multi-day portions of the trail are known. We were the only ones going the distance. We had the quiet riverside almost completely to ourselves.

Normally that was fine. But we hadn't passed anything that resembled a coffee shop since Abingdon, and we were ready for our morning tea and scones.

"We are being so stupid," I said. "Let's just look on our

phones!"

We turned on Sharon's iPhone since she had the best service—a full four bars, as she would for the entire trip. We opened Google Maps, entered "coffee shop," and waited for the familiar red dots to show the way.

No dots appeared.

We shook the phone. We tried the search a second time. I took the phone from Sharon and held it higher in the air, circling with it as though we were dance partners, in the hopes of finding a stronger connection. Nothing.

"Maybe Google Maps hasn't charted the countryside," Sharon suggested.

"Let's try 'restaurants,'" Linda offered, too hungry to throw in the towel.

Still nothing.

Thoughts of scones and a warm place to rest started slipping away. We hadn't seen anything but the river, fields, and trees for some time now.

*Why aren't we carrying snacks*, I chastised myself, deliberately overlooking how proud I had been when it occurred to me to travel so lightly. We didn't even have a change of slacks for the evening.

Meanwhile, Linda wasn't the only one who needed to stop. Sharon's knees were bothering her. It didn't help that it was cold and damp, nor that there weren't any benches on this stretch of shoreline. There were villages in all directions, but we didn't want to chance spending hours roaming muddy country lanes without coming across an open café.

"Wait a minute!" Sharon exclaimed, her eyes lighting up. "What are we thinking? This is England!"

She took back her phone and typed "P U B."

Bingo. Red lights dotted the map on the screen. Fifteen minutes later we were sitting in front of a cozy fire, inhaling the fresh aroma of what I could only assume was baking bread, and warming our cold, damp bodies next to the mesmerizing flicker of the flames. Flowers on the windowsills added still more color to the scene.

"We don't get many out-of-towners this time of year," said an attractive young woman, as she set down our tea. "Where are you from?"

Soon we were engaged in lively conversation. We learned that not many American do the trail—even in the summer—and that, other than the British, the most common nationalities seen along the river's banks are German, French, and Israeli.

We finished our food and drink and headed back to the trail, Linda's ankles retaped, Sharon's knees rejuvenated, and all of our bellies content. As the river came into view, I had the impression of reentering another, now-familiar world, a nature-lover's paradise where birdcalls were the loudest noises, swans glided gracefully around every river bend, and an occasional scull skimmed by.

Sheltered from civilization, for much of the day we could have just as easily been walking in an earlier century. In truth we were in the middle of a densely populated country, still within an hour of London and near the city of Reading. And we now had a better understanding of just how accessible to us the nearby hamlets and pubs were, whenever we needed to rest our weary feet or stop someplace to refuel.

# One Question

I was now walking with Linda and Sharon rather than taking space for myself, happy to be part of the conversation. Vast, flat fields extended on both sides of the river, boats at times moored on its banks. Fences occasionally meant passing through gates, sometimes scaring off a magpie or blackbird keeping watch.

Time flew as Sharon and I peppered Linda with questions about her term at the Federal Reserve Bank, fascinated to get this chance peek inside an organization that holds such sway over the world economy.

"So did you work in banking before serving on the board?" Sharon asked, surprised to learn about this chapter in Linda's career.

"No," Linda explained. "Each regional bank has nine directors, three of whom cannot be officers, directors, or employees of a financial institution. They can't even own stock in a bank, which would be seen as a conflict of interest. The idea is that we—the three directors not associated with a bank, Class C directors—solely represent the interests of the public.

"Class C directors serve two of their six-year terms as vice chair and the last two years as chair. Twice a year they present to the Federal Reserve Board of Governors their constituency's perspective on an assigned topic."

Linda went on to help us understand the curious and somewhat confounding line the Fed straddles between being a governmental and a private entity.

"The average American probably assumes that the Fed is part of the government—that it's our central bank. It sort of is, and it sort of isn't. Although it's true that the system as a whole is overseen by a central governing body in Washington, the system itself is decentralized, comprised of twelve regional banks that all have their own boards. And while it's also true, of course, that the government authorized creation of those banks, each is actually an independent, self-financed corporation in which both the federal government and member banks have an interest but no actual ownership."

It wasn't until later, alone in my hotel room and still pondering our conversation, that I would wonder whether—like me so many times in my own career—during her time at the Fed Linda hadn't usually been the only woman in the room.

Poking around online, I learned that until 1977 there had never even been a woman on the board of a regional bank. I also learned there had since been a lot of initiatives to change that—to give seats at the table to not only women but minorities as well. I was encouraged that things seemed better than a few decades ago, and I hoped they continued to improve.

"I'm feeling very lucky to have amazing women like you in my life," I said, once our conversation about the Fed had run its course.

"This is the first time I've felt interesting in a long time," Linda confessed, casting her gaze over the river like a fisherman had cast his line not long before. "I've felt so worthless and boring."

"Boring?" Sharon and I exclaimed in disbelief.

"Yeah," Linda said. "Bruce even told me I was."

She proceeded to share stories of a woman neither of us recognized, one with seemingly little in common with the driven, accomplished professional who had held such high-profile roles in the business world, someone who seemed the very embodiment of success. The version of herself she now shared, however, was the personal one, a woman shattered and insecure because, Bruce, her husband of such a short time, had—to be blunt—dumped her.

"First though," Linda explained, "I let him talk me into giving up my job and home in Minneapolis. He said he would take care of me financially if I moved to Rochester, so we could be together. Then he changed his mind—about my living in Rochester, about the marriage, about everything. So now I've lost a ton of money, both on my house and not one but two moves. Oh yeah, and I don't have a job."

Sharon and I were dumbfounded, Linda's stories reminding me that regardless of how interesting or strong we might appear to the outside world, behind the scenes the reality can be much more complicated—especially when intimate relationships come into play.

Linda was one of the most interesting people I knew. Tall and attractive, she beamed positive energy and was always open to new ideas and experiences. Who was this bastard, I thought, who exploited her vulnerabilities and made her feel boring? For the first time since Harold died, someone else's problem grabbed me, pulling me out of my protective shroud. Here and now it was Linda's pain I needed to deal with, not mine.

On the surface, her loss might have seemed less significant than my losing Harold. Someone who loved me profoundly was gone, his death leaving me empty, searching for my missing half. I had lost my soulmate of decades through no choice of his own. Linda, on the other hand, had only recently married her husband, and he had decided to leave of his own accord.

I could take comfort knowing deep inside that I walked with Harold's love even if he was not physically here. All I had to do was curl up on my right side, my arms cupping my body, to feel him wrapped around me, reaching out to console me. He was gone, but his love was not.

Linda didn't have any such comfort. Far from it, she must have felt as though she had climbed a steep cliff only to discover the top blocked with barbed wire, her climb for naught. Her ego shattered, utterly confused about how to move forward, she even found herself burdened by financial challenges that would require years to untangle. And it wasn't over. Her maybe-soon-to-be-ex threatened to cause her still more unhappiness.

"Now he's changed his mind again," she continued, her voice increasingly strained. "He wants to stay married after all and 'explore alternatives,' whatever the hell that's supposed to mean."

During the years that Harold struggled with his cancer, I was mostly present and strong, rolling with the punches and reveling in the joyous times between setbacks, times when we couldn't get enough of life's experiences. I deeply believe that his illness, in addition to being devastating, frightening, and, ultimately, terminal, was also a gift of life. We lived more fully in that time than I could have ever imagined.

Unlike Linda, I had time to prepare. And when I was sad, angry, or—worst of all—just plain terrified, I had help.

"What frightens you the most?" asked Kazumi, my latest therapist.

Short and of average weight, she had dark hair, smooth skin, and a gentle smile. We were meeting in the office she had downstairs in her home. Books lined walls of shelves, plants added color to corners, she and I sat in comfortable chairs. Alone with her in this welcoming space, I took a deep breath and relaxed.

It was about ten years into the illness that should have led to Harold's death long before. In spite of the fact that he hadn't gone into remission, that the cancer was still there, he was still alive—and we continued to fight. At the University of California at San Francisco, angels like Eric Small, head of research for urologic oncology—who always took the time to give Harold a hug—or his nurse practitioner, Tammy Rodvelt, heard Harold out, let me rage, and always had one more proposal, still more options, to extend our hope. And Harold's life.

Meanwhile Harold was evolving into an increasingly spiritual person. As his disease progressed, he spent days in silence at Spirit Rock, a world-renowned insight meditation center in Marin County. He also spent time at Commonweal Cancer Retreat in Bolinas, leading to his involvement with a women's cancer group. He forged such bonds with those women that they were among his very last visitors, circling his bed in his final days, offering support and holding space.

As for me, outwardly I seemed the same energetic person I had always been. Inside an abyss was opening.

I was terrified. I was starting to panic about Harold dying.

I had spent all those years taking care of him and making sure *he* was OK. One day it hit me: what was going to happen to *me*?

My one experience of watching someone lose their beloved was my mother. When she lost my father, the strong woman I had always known turned gray overnight. Her identity dissolved, and she became no one. What was it going to be like for me to lose my own sweetheart?

I had been to several therapists, all of whom were a waste of time. They asked stupid questions and told me what I should and should not be feeling. I stopped seeing one. And then another. And another.

Those failures didn't change the fact: I still needed help.

Kazumi didn't know if she should see me as a patient, because Harold and I were friends with her husband. She eventually overcame her hesitance. My previous experiences had made me a cynic, and I was impatient to see results. I told myself I'd try just a few visits with her.

As our first session got underway, we muddled around my concerns. Once more I found myself questioning whether our time together was going to do any good. Until a single question changed everything.

"When Harold dies, who will you be?"

"What?" I asked, staring at her, my eyes wide, my pulse racing.

"When Harold dies," she said slowly, deliberately, "who will you be?"

The world went hollow. The answer fell from my mouth before my mind could give it another thought.

"I will be the woman he loved."

Kazumi looked at me. She looked at her notebook. Silence filled the space between us. She looked back up at me.

"And?" she said, unhurried.

Suddenly there was no fear. No tension left in my body. Just calm.

"The woman he loved."

Not an epitaph, but a starting point.

That single realization relieved me of my terror, the fear that I might crash when Harold died. It was as if a door I had been holding shut with all my might burst open, revealing there had never been a monster hidden behind it.

It wasn't until much later that I figured out why, at least in part, the question had been so powerful—and the answer even more so. In that moment I understood—not just intellectually, but experientially, in the depths of my heart—that, though a time would come when he was no longer physically in this world, Harold would never leave me.

The session was over. I never went back. There was no need.

I did, however, continue to be amazed my conundrum had been resolved in a single visit. Kazumi had asked so few questions.

In the end, it only took one.

---

"You know," Linda continued, "I actually knew for a while that Bruce was very different from how he presented himself during our courtship. But I wanted it to work, so I adapted to his ways. He had great contacts all over the world. We took fabulous trips and had a lot of fun. I just ignored the warning signals. I don't know if I want to stay with him."

My eyes drawn to the river by the sound of lapping water, I spied a tall, sleek heron hiding among some reeds. Motionless, it didn't seem to mind the cold or gray.

"Well, if now he doesn't want a divorce," I asked, "what does he want?"

"He wants us to have a relationship like the one we had before we got married and I moved to Rochester. He says he wants to travel together. Honestly though, I don't know what he wants. It hurts my head to think about it."

"But what do *you* want?" Sharon asked.

Linda paused to gather her thoughts.

"You know, I came here thinking I would consider it, maybe try to make it work. But walking with the two of you is giving me time to think clearly. I'd rather be alone than stuck in this disaster I thought was the best I could do. I think he wanted me to feel inadequate and become dependent on him—he's even kept money he owes me. I can't believe I let someone do that, and I don't know how I was even considering going back. Besides, my son and daughter can't stand him."

"They've never liked him?" Sharon asked.

"No, they disliked him from the start."

"And this wasn't a clue?" I wondered.

"I thought they would come around."

Neither Sharon nor I said anything, wheels spinning in Linda's head.

I became lost in my own thoughts, my mind latching onto Linda's comments about Bruce wanting to make her financially dependent, about how he was supposed to take care of her but only ended up both costing and owing her money.

I began my life a poor refugee, at a time when everyone expected a woman to be dependent on a man. That included my mother.

"The man isn't in charge, Tania," she would insist, desperate for me to see things from her perspective, to adopt her model of survival, "but you have to let him *think* he is!"

My mother was a strong personality and a very intelligent woman. She used that intelligence to give men—my father, in particular—the impression they were in control. In reality, nearly without fail, at home things were done her way. She even managed the finances, although nobody on the outside had any idea.

That was never going to be me.

At age twelve I vowed I would always be financially independent. At age fifteen, my resolve became forever embedded, a hand on my flesh like a hot iron on my psyche.

My brother, his friend Val, and I were sitting in the back of our car, a Nash Rambler. My father was driving. Val and I had an innocent fondness for one another, obvious in our playful banter. Papa saw nothing funny about our rapport, disgusted by what he considered my shameless flirtation. While keeping one hand on the steering wheel, with the other he delivered a painful, soul-crushing smack.

The fun was over.

And so was our relationship.

From then on, not only was a wall erected between me and my father that wouldn't come down until after his death, but I refused to take another dime from my parents. Lying about my age, I got my first job, working in a delicatessen. At sixteen—well before the rest of my peers—I enrolled at the University of California, Berkeley. Even then, my resolve remained unfaltering: I never took another penny from my family. My father would not tell me what to do. Never again.

Neither did my conviction change when Harold and I married. I insisted we keep separate bank accounts, other than a joint one for household expenses. He wholeheartedly agreed.

I wanted to ensure my independence. Harold wanted to know he would be financially secure if one of us left the other. In their divorce, he had given almost everything to his wife, leaving him with the same net worth as me—except he was ten years older. In his mind, he had fallen way behind. If he divorced again, his life would be in unsalvageable ruin. So, for two very different reasons, we both thought keeping separate accounts was a great idea. At first.

One day a few months after we were married, Harold and I looked at each other and burst into laughter. In that moment, we both saw it: we'd been treating our marriage as if we were each putting the other through some sort of probationary period, like young new hires who had to prove their worth before being offered full-time positions.

The probationary period was over. So were separate finances.

"He really did make me believe I was boring, you know," Linda continued, both of us returning from our thoughts. "And besides, he's outrageously conservative politically."

"What?" I asked, amazed. "I can't imagine someone as progressive as you with someone like that."

"I just never talk politics with him," she explained. "And it never occurs to him to ask how I feel. He just rants about entitlements and makes nasty remarks about Obama.

What a jerk!"

"Linda, this doesn't sound like you at all," I remarked. "You deserve a soulmate, not someone with beliefs you abhor. What were you thinking?"

"Obviously, I wasn't," she replied, glancing at me with a knowing grin. "My therapist tells me that's the problem! When I get romantically involved, my brain goes to sleep, and my hormones take over."

"Well, there is something to be said for that," I said, chuckling ruefully. It had been a while since I'd thought about sexual attraction.

"I need to move on," Linda declared, after a moment of introspection. "I just needed to clear my head to figure it out. I'm done with Bruce."

# Reinvention

We were now walking alongside the water on a broad, relatively dry part of the trail. Tall, leafless trees lined the path and some boats appeared, two rowers in each.

Soon after, against a backdrop of overcast sky softened by puffy white clouds, the slate-gray roof and pointed spire of an old stone church emerged from a dense tangle of branches. In the foreground, four gothic arches of red brick spanned the river, each reflected on its surface, lending some color and even more grace to the picture-perfect scene.

We stopped to check the map.

We had arrived at Clifton Hampden. The brick, it turned out, belied the bridge's relatively young age—at least compared to some of the stone ones along the way. In 1867 the bridge had replaced a ferry service in operation since the early 1300s. It wasn't until hundreds of years later, in 1946, when the County Councils of Berkshire and Oxfordshire bought the bridge from its owners, that a toll was no longer necessary to make the jaunt from one side to the other.

Just before town we came upon a fourteenth-century inn called The Barley Mow, an old building with a thatched roof and a pub that served food. It was a good thing we arrived early and were able to get a table, because the place—a popular one, it turned out, for Sunday brunch—was soon mobbed by a lively crowd. Warmed by a cheery fire, which seemed to burn all the brighter given the room's dim lighting, dark paneling, and low ceiling, we joined in the festive mood and ordered wine with our meal. Linda, in particular, looked forward to it, hoping it might help numb the pain in her feet.

After a leisurely lunch and a chat with some locals, we headed on.

Sharon asked Linda about her college-age children: one an undergraduate, the other in law school. Linda explained that she wanted to support them fully, so they wouldn't have loans to pay off for years after graduation. She also funded her son's involvement with a legal project in Africa, as well as her daughter's year in London. Her children had grown up in a household where their parents had a difficult relationship, and I suspected Linda was trying to make it up to them. Regardless of the reason, she was committed to earning enough to maintain the lifestyle to which they were accustomed.

Sharon was a part-time executive coach, having given up her last full-time corporate job a few years earlier. She served on several boards of directors but was considering phasing out of business altogether as her interests moved elsewhere. A few years ago, she had completed a course in Asian Art at a prestigious museum in London.

As Sharon and Linda dove deeper into their discussion, I fell back, flooded with thoughts about my own career.

When Harold's illness led me to reassess my life, it quickly became clear I would not continue working. At forty-six, I had already had a full, varied, and successful career. He and I had always talked about eventually moving beyond our executive jobs, which, while deeply satisfying, left little time for our other passions—like family, hiking, and world travel. Harold had already made the transition. At fifty-five, he was done with the business world. I was running my third technology company, one I had successfully turned around and taken public. In the thick of a great career, I had just let my target retirement age of forty-five come and go.

But when I stopped to reflect, I had to acknowledge that, as satisfying as my work was, I was starting to get restless. Every three to five years, I simply reached a stage where I needed to make a major shift. Although I spent the first fourteen years of my professional life at one company, I never held the same job there more than three years. I also took a year off for study and several extended leaves of absence to travel. As I came to the end of my fourth year at my current company, Harold's diagnosis merely precipitated a decision I soon would have reached on my own: I was done.

I thought my initial reinvention would be as a writer. I have always loved mysteries and imagined a series about a feisty young woman who lands in a cheap hotel in San Francisco's notorious Tenderloin district. My first cut had her running into a scared prostitute outside a tattoo parlor at McAllister and Jones. That was as far as she—and I—got.

My writing career would have to wait. It turned out that being an executive was too deeply ingrained. Soon I was helping other writers, launching a literary society in Healdsburg.

Several years followed of involvement on various boards, until I finally moved completely out of that work to spend my time on other pursuits, including photography, traveling, and starting a non-profit to help more kids graduate from our public high school. I could deal with the challenges of extremely high drop-out rates; I no longer had a passion for business.

Returning from my thoughts, I heard Linda and Sharon further ahead conversing about their own passions. I picked up my pace and rejoined them.

Linda was explaining to Sharon that her Federal Reserve contacts, along with the other boards she served on, led to an ongoing stream of opportunities.

"I'm interested in a mix of startups, where I can share in equity, and boards of larger businesses, where I can get paid well now. And I need to figure it out in the next year or so, because after that my age will start to be an issue."

She raised an important point. I served on my first board of directors when I was in my early thirties. At the time, that was absurdly young.

As a young director, one of my biggest issues was dealing with directors too old to be effective but—since they had been on the board forever—with too much seniority to be asked to resign. At the time, there were far fewer regulations about who could serve on boards, and for how long, than there are now. Thankfully, things have improved a lot since I left behind the boardroom. Most companies now have term and age limits, and seventy is a commonly mandated retirement age. Linda was approaching sixty-six.

I reflected on the beginning of my executive career and couldn't help but laugh at how old Sharon, Linda, and I would have seemed to me then—*would have*, because at the time there were no role models like us. Women were all but invisible in corporate boardrooms and executive positions. I spent my entire career with men. They were my colleagues, my competitors, my bosses, and, when I became a

CEO, my board members.

At that point some of them also became a new sort of peers, inviting me to be part of a "CEO roundtable," a group of ten technology company CEOs who met twice a year to share business and life experiences. It became my most important support group. A CEO has a whole company reporting to them and reports to a board of directors—but has no one at their own level. There was nobody with whom I could be completely candid, openly share fears and aspirations. The Roundtable members became among the most important people in my life.

Thinking about it now, it was hard to believe we had been meeting for more than thirty years—and counting. Every one of the group flew to California for Harold's memorial. Most of them flew with me to Patagonia the following November to celebrate my first Thanksgiving as a single woman.

Until a few years ago, when my friend Judy joined, even my Roundtable friends were all men. When the very few of us women in the corporate world did find each other, we developed strong bonds, sharing the unique experience of being successful in a man's world. I laughed again, remembering one incident that illustrated that experience well.

I was running the Business Office at Control Data. The president of the International Division invited me to a meeting with the Japan country manager, who had come to headquarters to present the business strategy for his country. When the meeting was over, I stayed around to see if I could be of any help. Instead of talking to me about the business, he explained that in Japan, women—especially young women such as myself, not even thirty years old—

walked two steps behind men. Unshaken, I thanked him and left, deciding he wasn't worth my time.

A few minutes later there was a knock at my open office door. I looked up, surprised to see the same man. Gesturing for him to take a seat, I wondered what else I was about to learn about traditional Japanese culture.

"Is it true, Romanov-*san*, that you control the budgets for all new technology investments?"

It wasn't lost on me that he suddenly knew my name and had used the Japanese honorific -*san*.

"Yes, I do."

"So, we would need your approval to launch the projects I presented upstairs?"

"You would," I replied.

"Ah. I see." He shifted uneasily in the chair, beads of sweat gathering on his brow. "I would like you to visit us in Japan and hear more details about these projects."

"Would I have to walk a few steps behind?"

I couldn't resist.

"You know, Romanov-*san*," he began, almost pleading, "I have two daughters, and I confess they refuse to walk behind."

"I see."

"Maybe we could start our relationship again," he said, standing, bowing, and presenting me a business card with both hands outstretched.

As soft earth buffered my every step, a gust of wind momentarily drawing my attention back to my surroundings, to an aroma of rich dirt, dry leaves, and decaying trunks and branches, to the pleasing sight of the smooth river to my left, another memory surfaced.

Working for the same company, I was now living in a

small town near Geneva, traveling around Europe providing customer support. One day my boss was on a call with a client in Holland.

"I'm sorry to have to tell you this," my boss explained, hesitating, fearing how the client would take the news, "but I'm going to send you a woman." His forehead rippled like corrugated metal, his ordinarily pale face became flush. The muscles in his neck bulged as though on display.

Muttering came like static from the receiver, in response to which my boss insisted, "Yes, a woman—and a young one at that. But you have to trust me. She's our best. She can solve your problems. I have a guy I could send, but I don't think he'd be much help."

The conversation continued, alternating between prolonged semi-silences in which I could only guess how to interpret the faint, indecipherable voice from Holland, followed by still more reassurances from my boss, who was practically wiping his brow. It was all I could do to contain myself, but—biting down hard on my tongue—I did.

"How could you apologize for my being a woman!" I demanded, before the phone was even back on the cradle. "How could you say that?"

"I know, I know," he clamored, covering his face with his hands, as though to hide his shame. "But, Tania, I had to—it was for your benefit. If I had sent a woman without letting him know first, he might have sent you right back. Without the heads-up, he never would have believed you were the company's best technical person to resolve his issues. He probably wouldn't have even given you a chance."

It took me a minute to calm down. Once I did, I got it. My boss was on my side. He was helping me navigate challenges I still struggled to understand.

By the time I was in my early thirties, I did understand. I was now a general manager whose businesses included the Military Contracting Division, a secretive world of tough guys and hush-hush projects requiring government clearance. The crusty guy who ran the division was a retired career-military officer, whose macho, small-minded sense of self precluded having a woman for a boss.

"Can I just say something before we start?" he asked, as I was about to give his first performance review. "Off the record?"

"Sure," I said, bracing myself.

"Well, Tania, it's not just that you're a woman that makes this difficult for me. I could almost deal with that, I think." He paused, attempting to choose his next words carefully, but unable to hold back. "But for God's sake, you're younger than my son!"

I looked at him without a word, prolonging the silence. Then I smiled.

"Dean, if you don't think you're too old for the job, I don't have a problem with your son's age."

---

For four miles the trail stayed on the right bank of the river, following its gentle curves. When not reminiscing or engaged with Sharon and Linda, my mind was calm. I enjoyed the swans, the shadows thrown by the trees, the feeling of my legs moving toward a novel destination. I enjoyed when I wasn't thinking much at all, not about the past, about Harold, about loss.

Some hills rose up ahead, including one topped with a distinctive "clump" of trees. Hence the name the hill shared with its neighboring pair: the Wittenham Clumps. What's more, the trees crowning them weren't just any trees: they were the oldest beech-tree plantings in England, dating all the way back to the 1740s. Amidst their tall, pale trunks, a hollow named the Money-Pit was said to conceal a treasure trove guarded by a raven. I couldn't help but think that at least partly explained why the Clumps attracted more than 200,000 visitors a year.

The magnificent beeches still visible on the horizon, we approached a small lock. We crossed it, following the trail to other side of the river and closing in on our final destination of the day: the White Hart in Dorchester.

Not long after we were standing in front of a charming three-story, half-timbered building topped by three gables. "1691" was spelled out in the façade brick, presumably the year the structure was built.

Ready to rest our weary feet, we headed for the lobby. The interior of the hotel was an elegant, welcoming mix of exposed wood beams, brick, and stone.

After quick showers, we reconvened downstairs, where a roaring fire warmed a small bar. Surprised to find it mostly empty, the bartender confirmed it was normally much busier on weekends. More importantly, yes, we were delighted to hear, he could make us mojitos with fresh mint.

After enjoying our drinks, we returned to the front desk to ask Lizzie, the friendly, knowledgeable young woman who had checked us in, for a recommendation about a good next stop for our walk. When she mentioned the Miller of Mansfield Inn, I recognized it as a favorite of Sue's. The only problem was that it was in the town of Goring, a questionably long walk. After a brief discussion—perhaps emboldened by the alcohol—we decided to go for it.

Lizzie's round face lit up, her dark eyes suddenly aglow. "In that case, you must stop for lunch at The Beetle and Wedge—it's on your way!"

"Why is everyone talking about The Beetle and Wedge?" I asked. Several people along the trail had already told us about it, purportedly not to be missed.

"Oh, trust me—you'll love lunch there!" Lizzie insisted, thick eyebrows raised and ordinarily smooth forehead wrinkled with enthusiasm.

Trust her we did, grateful when she booked us a table for one thirty the next day.

# Staggered Maturities

Monday, the third day of our walk, we hit our stride.

Everyone felt good, physically and emotionally. The weather was cold when we set out, but soon warmed enough for us to shed gloves and hats and extra layers.

I hung back, taking my own space, relaxed and enjoying the feel of the soft, damp trail beneath my feet. When I stopped to watch a group of brown swans—the teen-age version of the ugly duckling of childhood stories—I turned to point them out to Harold. Except Harold wasn't there. The cygnets' graceful parents coasted further from shore, like extras on a Hollywood set paid to create atmosphere for passers-by.

I resumed my stroll.

A moment earlier, I had hoped to see Harold behind me. Now, I longed for him to be in front of me. When he was alive, that was never an option. He was too tall. Like a plant withering in the long shadow cast by his lanky, towering body, I couldn't see the sun. Or anything else. I always walked in front.

I smiled, unexpectedly reminded of a favorite memory.

The first year of our marriage, Harold and I traveled so much for our jobs that we spent little time together. Since this came as no surprise, we accepted it for what it was—it caused no tension. We simply did our best to connect whenever and wherever our travels permitted.

When we both found ourselves with upcoming trips to Japan—his for three weeks, mine for one—we jumped at the opportunity to spend time together in Tokyo, taking two days off from work and exploring the city. I'll never forget the beautiful gardens where we strolled, the tranquil, reflective ponds traversed by storybook bridges and landscaping manicured with the meticulous detail so characteristic of the Japanese.

Neither will I forget the hilarious scene that played out whenever we entered a building. Shocked and amazed by Harold's 6'6" frame, concerned women—young and old alike—would rush to his aid, urging him to bend down, for fear he would hit his head. I lost count of how many times I saw women get on their tiptoes to protect Harold's imperiled noggin. And whenever their benevolent efforts presented the opportunity, they couldn't resist touching the top of his head, sending me barreling over with laughter.

Several paces down the trail, Sharon was telling Linda what it was like to be in Iran at the end of the Shah's government, as well as her jobs that followed. I listened with half an ear. Unlike with Linda, I had stayed in touch with Sharon through the experiences she now shared. They were new to Linda, however, and she was deeply interested, especially in hearing more about Sharon's transition from full-time work to part-time consulting and serving on boards.

When I walked with my friends in California, business never came up. Most of them had little knowledge of my background outside of our small-town community. Sharon, Linda, and I, however, were all going through career and post-career transitions. It was only natural—if not inevitable—that we'd talk about such things.

I laughed as I realized I had mentally drawn an analogy of the three of us to a laddered bond portfolio with "staggered maturities." Perhaps I was not as far removed from my business background as I liked to think! The timing of these bonds, I posited, had less to do with our ages and more with our life choices: having children late, staying single, a spouse's illness. All of us had dived fully into our jobs and were extremely lucky in our success. But as each of our careers reached "maturity," we had a shared desire to pursue other interests and live full, well-rounded lives.

I suspected that Sharon, sandwiched between my stage and Linda's, was enjoying the opportunity to think about where her life was heading. It would be easy for her to revisit the excitement of leadership opportunities or help a non-profit find its way. But she was approaching another phase, with few models for how to proceed.

"Maybe guidebooks just aren't our thing because we've had so few examples to guide us through life," Linda had joked earlier.

"Harold always resisted the word *retirement*," I commented, picking up my pace and rejoining Sharon and Linda. We were passing through the outskirts of the town of Benson, large boats moored in a succession of docks.

"Why's that?" Sharon asked.

"He said it implied that life was about work," I explained, "and that it made it sound like leaving behind a career was analogous to being put out to pasture."

Crossing a long metal walkway over the Benson lock, we marveled at this, yet another impressive structure. And as we savored the exhilaration of standing in wide-open space in the middle of the river, powerful cascades created by the lock once more raging below us, we launched into a lively discussion.

Our experiences of this stage of life were dramatically different from the preconceived notions with which we'd been raised. We were supposed to retire at sixty-five. We were supposed to transition into an easy, predictable life of much leisure but little purpose. Except that didn't work for us. We were defining life paths as we went.

Sharon had heard our intentional approach to our next phases referred to as the "Portfolio Life." I immediately took to the idea, later learning that those very words were trademarked. Key to this concept was that successful people could "continue living lives of significance" while taking time to rest, recharge, and enjoy the fruit of their labors.

"So many people struggle to retire," said Sharon, "because they don't know what to do with themselves. They can't find a passion to replace their work."

"It's so true!" I agreed. "But we certainly don't fall into that category!"

"Are you kidding?" chimed in Linda. "Between the three of us, there aren't enough hours in the day for all the things we want to do!"

A V-shaped flock of geese honked overhead, making their way across the winter sky.

"I do feel a need to let go of striving as a key driver, though," Sharon admitted. "It's how I grew up measuring myself. I was always setting external goals. I don't want to get satisfaction that way anymore, but it's hard."

She took a deep breath, pausing to reflect.

"I like being recognized as successful more than I want to admit," she continued. "It's comfortable. But I don't want to fall into taking on another board just because it's prestigious or pays well—even if it's fascinating. I want to get beyond that."

"What do you want to do?" asked Linda. "Even if I didn't need the money, I wouldn't be ready to give up this life. I still find it so stimulating intellectually."

"I can tell," said Sharon. "and I want to find something that stimulates me as well. But in a new way."

"To be honest, right now I need the familiarity," Linda confessed. "It keeps me from dwelling on what happened with Bruce. I get to travel and meet people—and it helps keep my ego intact."

"In fact," she continued, "it's why I'm able to be here with you guys. It was thanks to my board meeting in Denmark and my plans to visit my daughter in London that we started thinking about this trip!"

A short while later, the appearance of another noteworthy bridge prompted us to pull out the guidebook—quickly proving Linda's earlier point: guidebooks were not our forte. I was used to navigating with topographic maps and compasses or, more recently, a GPS. What's more, I normally hiked in the wilderness. I was confident of my orienteering ability in the middle of nowhere; walking through towns full of people was different—I had never even used a guidebook. It didn't help that ours traveled from "the sea to the source," the opposite direction we were headed. It was hopelessly confusing. Over and over I turned the book upside down in frustration, eliciting guffaws from my friends. Eventually, we settled on a timeworn technique: we ignored the book—for the most part anyway.

True, we occasionally looked at the red line in the Sharp guide that indicated the trail. Unlike the other book, this one headed the direction we were going, clearly indicating which side of the river we should be on. We also used Google maps periodically to confirm exactly where we were in the moment, which was how we now discovered we were approaching Wallingford.

As for the bridge that gave us the heads-up, it was built of a familiar gray stone and comprised of three arches—the middle taller than the two on either side. Perhaps owing to the bridge's medieval origins and changes to the river's course in the centuries since, a series of additional arches supported it over a wide, grassy plain. A balustrade on top added a touch of elegance, ensuring that the couple of bikers crossing it now didn't get too close to the edge.

Although the bridge no doubt had a colorful history, we were more intrigued by another aspect of Wallingford's past.

"Didn't Agatha Christie live here?" Linda said. "I feel like I read something about her in connection with this town."

"I thought it was something to do with *Midsomer Murders*," I replied, recalling a BBC series that Harold and I had enjoyed on Netflix.

Soon we were in the town itself. The most bustling one we had visited since Oxford, its main road was lined with lovely old buildings and shops. Wallingford felt like a fun place to spend some time.

I looked at my phone: it was close to noon. We had lunch reservations at The Beetle and Wedge at 1:30.

Up ahead, a tourist office sat on an island in the middle of the road, as though grateful not to get carried away by traffic. We walked inside, where we learned the restaurant was in the town of Moulsford, a little over an hour's walk away.

A half hour didn't seem like enough time to explore Wallingford.

"Are there buses or taxis to Moulsford?" I asked.

"They're not waiting out there for fun," cackled the woman in the tourist office. In her early sixties, she seemed like quite a fuddy-duddy, as though she might have once been a stern headmistress. She gestured to three London-style black cabs outside the window, where a bus was also within sight.

While the woman and I went out to talk to one of the taxi drivers, Linda and Sharon found some information about Agatha Christie, who had in fact lived in Wallingford for many years. They learned that more books by Agatha Christie—four billion—have been sold than by any other author in history, except, well, God (the Bible has done surprisingly well). She had certainly been important in my life: I learned Italian by reading her in translation, a significant improvement from the Nancy Drew books I used learning French!

From 1934 to 1976 Christie lived in Wallingford with her husband, archaeologist Max Mallowan. She is buried in nearby Cholsey. And I was right: *Midsomer Murders* was sometimes filmed in Wallingford, with Detective Chief Inspector Barnaby often wandering around town.

I had to see Christie's house. Sharon and Linda were more interested in exploring. We decided to go our separate ways.

After strolling through a mile of antique stores, coffee shops, and pubs and restaurants, I found what I was looking for. A wrought-iron gate between two large, manicured hedges opened onto a gravel yard. A short distance away, a three-story Queen Anne house nestled among mature trees laid unquestionable claim to a large plot, which extended all the way to the Thames, out of sight on the back side of the property.

The home's façade was comprised of two colors of brick, the predominant gray complemented by red around the five windows, each of which had white frames. The door, perfectly centered between the ground-floor windows, was also painted an immaculate white. Three dormers peeked out of a terracotta-tile roof, behind and at one end of which chimneys took to a cloudless sky. Finally, as if to allay any lingering doubts, a blue plaque next to the door confirmed I was in the right place.

I felt a surge of excitement, as the reality hit that so many of my favorite books had been written in this very house. Countless times, Agatha herself had walked out that door, passed through the gate on which my own hand now rested. I longed for her to step outside now. I had so many questions.

But Agatha's time here had long ago come and gone. And it was time for me to be on my way, too. I had lunch plans.

As I approached the taxi stand an hour after separating from my friends, I noticed something awry: there were no taxis.

"They must have just got customers," Linda offered, as she approached from the opposite direction.

"Oh yeah," I agreed. "Another one will show up soon."

Sharon had arrived shortly before and was already double-checking with the woman inside the tourist office.

"They come and go," she reassured her. "You know how it is. Sit tight and they'll be back in a jiffy!"

A few minutes later, still no taxis.

The clock was ticking.

I went inside and asked if we could call a cab. The woman looked in several folders and found a few numbers. None of local cabbies answered. She finally got a hold of a driver in a neighboring town who agreed to come get us, but he was twenty minutes away—and couldn't leave for another twenty still.

"We're going to miss lunch," Linda lamented.

"Even if we miss our 1:30 reservation," Sharon agreed, fearing the worst, "they won't seat us after 2:00."

We called the restaurant. They agreed to hold our table until two—but, as Sharon had rightly surmised—no later. They didn't have any flexibility, because they needed to close the kitchen to prepare for dinner. We asked if anyone could pick us up, but there was no one on hand but waitstaff and kitchen crew.

Just then a bus pulled up across the street. The passengers exited, and the driver turned off the motor. I bolted outside to talk to him.

"Do you go to Moulsford?" I asked, out of breath.

"Sure do."

Reserved, with gray hair, slightly sagging jowls, and clear blue eyes, his tone suggested my question was a tedious one; one to which the answer should have been obvious.

"When do you leave?"

"Two o'clock."

Not the answer I was hoping for.

"Is there another bus before that?"

"Lady," he laughed, as though my questions were only getting more absurd, "I'm the only bus that goes to Moulsford."

"My friends and I were planning to take a taxi to The Beetle and Wedge, but the taxis have all disappeared."

"They usually take lunch now, like I do."

"None of them mentioned that when I asked earlier about getting a ride. We've got a 1:30 reservation, and they stop serving at 2:00." I didn't know why I was telling him all this—maybe for no other reason than that he was listening.

"You have a reservation at The Beetle and Wedge?" he asked, unsure he'd heard right.

"Yes. Everyone has been telling us how great it is, but we've never been."

"Neither have I. But I'd sure like to take my wife sometime." He relaxed into his seat, as though he no longer found our conversation quite so insufferable.

"Where are your friends?" he asked.

"Right over there." I pointed across the street, where Sharon and Linda had collared someone else for advice.

"Tell them to come here. I'll take you."

"Really?"

"Yes, but hurry! We barely have time to make it."

I shouted across the street, and Sharon and Linda came running. We all jumped onto the red double-decker, and the driver practically peeled out, throwing us off balance even more than his startling generosity already had. We clustered around his booth.

"I can't believe you are doing this!" Linda shouted over the noise of changing gears.

"Neither can I," he called back, "but I can't let you miss this opportunity. I'll have time to come back and eat lunch before I have to go again."

Ten minutes later we were at our destination, which

shortly before had seemed almost out of reach.

"It's just down the hill. Enjoy your lunch!"

"We can't thank you enough," I said, pulling out some money.

"You don't need to pay me," he insisted, his hands not moving from the big steering wheel, the smell of exhaust creeping in through the open door.

I couldn't let his good deed go unrewarded.

"Take your wife to lunch at the Beetle and Wedge on your next day off!" it occurred to me to suggest, after much back and forth.

A big grin crossed his face, and he finally accepted my gift.

I stepped off the bus and walked down the hill, catching up with Linda and Sharon. We had heard the restaurant described as an old boathouse on the water. What we found instead was an updated brick structure topped with multiple pitched gables of wood and glass, a striking combination of old and new.

Inside made even more of an impression. Large skylights let in abundant light, and the entire back wall was lined with tall windows overlooking the river. Exposed beams buttressed the gables. Different sizes and tones of stone pavers covered the floor, and the brick we'd seen outside was exposed inside as well. Tables were positioned with ample space for privacy, set with white tablecloths and fine china and silver. Tasteful flower arrangements colored and perfumed the room which, like so many other locales where we'd dined and drank, included a fireplace kept aflame by a neatly arranged pile of wood.

Except for an elegant couple who spoke softly in what seemed like "posh" English, the room was empty. The couple fell silent the moment we appeared.

Perhaps that was because, in our excitement for having made it on time, we were chattering and laughing like schoolgirls. It couldn't help that we were covered in mud, loaded down with daypacks, trail shoes, and layers of clothing.

When a black-vested waiter appeared, I could only assume he was going to politely inform us the kitchen was closed—a roundabout way of saying there was no way he was seating us looking like we did, no doubt in complete and utter violation of their dress code.

"Ladies!" he grinned, opening both arms in welcome, "We're so happy you made it!"

A good-looking, late twentysomething, his dark hair was cut short, his smile as bright as it was irresistible. Nothing about him betrayed the high-end snobbery we had feared our lowbrow appearances might elicit in this sort of locale.

He asked how we had pulled off the seemingly impossible, as a young woman approached to take our gear. The discrete couple perked up, listening to every last detail of our odyssey—the woman even interjecting a couple of questions—before our host showed us to our table. Soon we were sipping the house specialty, kir royales.

"We thought this was just an old boat house," I shared with the waiter, as he handed us each a menu. "But this place is gorgeous!"

"That is so kind of you to say!" he said, as though genuinely touched. "The building was built sometime before 1860, and it was in fact a working boathouse. It was used for the ferry until 1967, when the last ferrywoman retired."

"Really?" I said. "A ferry*woman* no less! It's so interesting to hear about the history of these places."

"In that case," our host continued, "you might also be interested to know that this very stretch of river is not only immortalized in *The Wind in the Willows*, but also in Jerome K. Jerome's *Three Men in a Boat*."

I didn't know the second book, but I certainly knew the first.

"And what about the name?" Linda wondered.

"Yeah," I interjected, "hopefully you don't have a problem with infestations!"

"No, no, fear not!" the young man laughed. "Besides being an insect, *beetle* is a term for a maul used with a wedge to split wood."

"You mean like a hammer?" clarified Sharon.

"Exactly."

After our new friend left us to look over the menu, a quiet descended upon the table. For now, we had all talked enough. I took a sip of my kir royale, savoring that we had made it and unspeakably grateful for the kindness of strangers.

After a much longer lunch than we'd been led to believe would be possible, we returned to the trail. This section continued all the way to Goring.

We passed an occasional house on the opposite bank. Once in a while there were more docks with handsome boats, no doubt impatient for the fun-filled excursions that would start up again in spring. Eventually we came across another lock, though this one we didn't cross.

As I walked, the air still warm, a light breeze coming

off the river, for the first time it occurred to me that I didn't miss my camera. This was unusual—almost unheard of, in fact. Since Harold's death, photography had become even more of an interest, a way not only to spend time but to fill the emptiness. I walked, as though afraid of what might happen if I stopped. I photographed, as though afraid of what I might see if, instead of outside, I turned my gaze inward.

And that external gaze had shifted. For years my focus was landscapes. When I lost Harold, from one day to the next I started shooting images of strangers, using my lens to fill the empty spot beside me with their faces. My images were overtaken by people, their eyes meeting mine in mutual recognition.

As Linda, Sharon, and I followed the Thames, there were moments when I was tempted to capture an image: a misty morning, a play of light on water, the serious, determined expressions of rowers. But the desire to create was fleeting. Instead, scenes flowed through me, the inspiration curative like medicine: it worked its magic then dissolved, leaving random, enduring impressions that uplifted my body and soul.

Not feeling the need to stop and capture the moments allowed me to simply be in them. I was able to relax into a comfortable rhythm. As the days had progressed, I'd been feeling increasingly calm and content.

As for the present, after a succession of four small, wooded islands, yet again a bridge heralded our impending arrival at the day's destination.

The Goring and Streatley Bridge was built in 1923 and has two spans, each meeting in an island. I was reminded of the Bay Bridge at home. This one, however, was on a scale many times smaller, consisting of timber struts that supported a metal roadway.

We crossed the river and were soon in Goring. Our hotel, the Miller of Mansfield, turned out to be a traditional, rambling brick structure. Its footprint following the angle in the road, the hotel looked as if it might have originally been two, if not three, buildings, now a united whole. One section had two stories; another three. Both were topped with a terracotta shingle roof and had multi-paned windows with white wood trim. Multiple brick chimneys betrayed at least as many fireplaces inside.

Dark wood floors creaked as we walked into the lobby, heading straight for the reception. We were exhausted, looking forward to cleaning up and regrouping for the next day. First though, we needed some information.

The young blonde woman at the reception confirmed our suspicions: we didn't need to spend time in the large city of Reading. Instead, we would pass right through it and go all the way to Sonning.

"Sonning is such a lovely village," she offered with an eager smile, her clear blue eyes sparkling. "And the Great House Hotel is a nice place to stay, with reasonable rates."

She also told us about a restaurant in Reading, in the middle of the river.

"You can make it in time for a late lunch," she said.

Our plans for the next day, Tuesday, were set. That evening, for the first time since setting out on our adventure, our trio would temporarily disband. Sharon would leave for a night in London. After attending a board meeting, she would return to the trail late Wednesday.

"And what about Wednesday?" I asked the receptionist.

"If you're going to Henley, naturally you want to stay at the Phyllis Court Club."

"The Phyllis Court Club?" I wondered.

"Oh, you mean you've never heard of it? So sorry—I shouldn't have assumed. You will love it. It's right on the river, where they hold the annual rowing regatta."

"Sounds good to us," I said, as she picked up the phone to make the reservation.

# Curiosity

We got off to a good start on Tuesday. We were well rested, and the temperature was mild. The sky was overcast, but the scenic countryside inspired and motivated us.

That all changed when, after a few hours, the trail headed away from the water and into a suburb.

By now it was past noon. We were tired and hungry. And after being spoiled by the rural beauty of the last few days, none of us found appealing the urban area slowly engulfing us. We just wanted to skip it.

We wandered onto a main road, walking toward Reading. We hoped either to find a bus or call a taxi to get us back to the countryside as soon as possible.

Doing so proved difficult. We got confused about which direction we were headed. The taxi driver we called already had rides scheduled, and he wasn't sure when he could come.

But then a big, red double-decker—something we didn't expect to see here on the outskirts of town—appeared out of nowhere. It pulled to a stop right in front of us.

We asked the driver if he was heading to Reading. With a nod, he confirmed he was. We climbed onboard and headed toward town.

"Saved by the double-decker bus—again!" I laughed.

Stop by stop, the bus filled up. Flat, drab, unremarkable, if we hadn't been driving on the "wrong" side of the road, we might have been in the nondescript outskirts of a town in the American Midwest. We flew by warehouses and car dealerships, storage facilities and office parks.

Just as it was getting unbearably full—people who didn't have seats standing shoulder to shoulder, jostled by the motion—the bus turned left and came to a stop. We got off and walked onto a bridge overlooking the river. Below, we saw an island that might have been artificial, given the metal barrier along its periphery, seemingly protecting it from crumbling into the water. Following a staircase down to a red walkway with glass railings, we crossed it and found ourselves in an unlikely refuge amidst the chaos of the city.

More swans than we had seen for the entire trip congregated just upriver, others circled below. As crowds fed them, the birds fought over crumbs and scones and heels of bread—somehow still maintaining their grace and poise.

The gray skies began to clear while we looked for the restaurant. It shouldn't have been difficult to find, given that there were only two buildings on the island. Yet somehow we didn't see any signs or an open entrance.

Eventually, at the end of the larger building, we came upon a staircase. We climbed it, entering a very large, very empty restaurant—which, we now learned, was appropriately named the Island Restaurant. Enchanted by walls of glass overlooking the river, we approached them to behold the views. Children played on the grassy shore, birds circled in the air, historic buildings lined the neighboring streets on both sides of the water. From our privileged vantage point, Reading suddenly seemed much more charming.

A waiter politely watched while we took it all in. What we didn't realize was that lunch was almost over—until we'd shown up, he had been about to leave.

"No, no! Don't go anywhere!" he insisted, as we headed for the door. "We would be happy to fix something for you!"

The pitcher of water was emptied almost as soon as it landed on the table. Our ravenous appetites ensured the basket of Italian bread suffered a similar fate, as did the burger, salmon, and pizza that followed. Our hunger didn't stop us from relishing the views, however, nor from appreciating the kindness of yet another stranger who had gone out of his way—extending his workday—to see that we were taken care of.

---

After lunch Sharon headed to the train station, bound for her meeting in London. Linda needed a break from walking—and perhaps from the never-ending companionship—and caught a taxi to Sonning. I savored the unexpected opportunity to walk alone.

I followed the right bank of the river, musing that only a country with so much rain could afford so much green lawn. Presently, though, there wasn't any rain, and the sun brought out scores of families onto the waterway's verdant banks. The clamorous city we bussed through earlier felt like another world far, far away.

A short while later I passed some office parks. When I noticed that Oracle and other Silicon Valley high tech companies had regional headquarters here, I was again reminded of my past life in that world. It seemed so distant now. Come to think of it, even my current life in California felt distant, almost abstract, as though it were someone else's.

Linda and Sharon might not have been with me as I

continued walking, but I wasn't alone. Harold seized the opportunity to be at my side, reminding me of the many companionable days we spent hiking. We were well matched in our love of exercise, of the outdoors, of adventure and exploration. All the same, there was no denying we had radically different approaches to them.

Harold was a planner. He would research where we were going, then loved to discuss the options: how long we could hike; where we might end; what highlights we didn't want to miss. I was happy to let him do all the research, though naturally I would speak up if I had strong feelings about his proposed itineraries. And I did my part, planning the travel logistics to and from wherever we were going.

Long before we got into the car or boarded a plane, Harold would have studied the terrain we'd be hiking, considered the challenges, and, as needed, trained in preparation. I would usually join him, per the constraints of my jobs, often enjoying the training as much as the trip itself.

When the time came to go, he would carefully fold and pack his beloved topographic hiking maps—including a few extras that might prove helpful, just in case. He would have planned every last detail of the trip, including the goal. There was always a goal.

I didn't care about the goal. I never have. Unlike my sweetheart, I didn't need to reach a particular peak or behold a famous overlook or dip my toe into a hard-to-reach lake. Confounding, given my success in the highly goal-oriented world of business. Or, maybe not, considering a curious, defining trait of my own: I can't bear the thought of not seeing what's around the next corner, beyond the upcoming curve, just over the last step. I have an almost obsessive need to know where the next challenge might lead.

My curiosity is endless. Exceptional or ordinary, whatever comes next is always worthwhile—I'm never disappointed. It helps that I have a preternatural ability to overlook sore feet, exhaustion, nausea, hunger, and anything else that might otherwise stand in my way.

Harold had goals. I had curiosity. We reached the same peaks.

Including Mount Whitney.

---

Long before we met, Harold had attempted to summit the highest mountain in North America. Now known by the name given to it by the indigenous Koyukon people, Denali, at the time the mountain—which also happens to be the world's tallest from base to peak on land—was known as Mount McKinley, after the twenty-fifth president of the United States.

Before Harold was able to reach the 20,310-foot peak, he was forced to turn back.

Many years into his illness, he was no longer strong enough to ponder another attempt of Denali or a return to the Himalayas. All the same, somewhere along the way another mountain called out to him, as though issuing one last, unforeseen challenge, a reminder that he was in fact still very much alive—and extending an invitation to prove it.

Once Harold heard the call, his mind was made up. While there was still a chance his body could pull it off, we had to climb Mount Whitney. It wasn't the tallest mountain in the world, but at 14,505 feet it was the highest in the contiguous United States. And we wouldn't even have to leave the state to get to it.

We would, however, have to train.

That was when Harold the Planner took over.

We would start our climb at the Whitney Portal trailhead, located at 8,374 feet of elevation. From there, the ascent would entail a gain of 6,000 feet to the summit. Naturally, Harold reasoned, we couldn't just show up and do a 6,000-foot climb. We would have to undertake some real conditioning.

The problem was that we were in the Bay Area, where there aren't mountains anywhere near that tall. No matter, Harold insisted, we would work with what we had.

He decided the first peak to tackle was one we could reach from sea level: Mount Tamalpais, locally known as Mt. Tam, in Marin County, just across the Golden Gate Bridge from San Francisco.

The morning of our first training hike, we left the car at a beach where a trail led up the mountain. The Pacific slowly stretching out beneath us, its mighty roar soon inaudible, we walked in and out of forests and through golden grasslands. Our feet traversed dusty trails, rock stairs that seemed they'd never end—our thighs and calves burning, our lungs pumping—and redwood bridges that squeaked under our weight. Creeks trickled, ravens sounded alarms, and red-tailed hawks unleashed their piercing cries, circling on thermals high in an immaculate blue sky. We saw lizards and coyotes, woodpeckers and deer. We breathed in the invigorating scents of eucalyptus and bay; the intoxicating, sweet aroma of sagebrush.

More than three hours later, we reached the peak, collapsing onto some boulders and taking in the stunning vistas of Marin, the East Bay, and the City, as well as the

Pacific. Our celebration, however, was short-lived.

"How'd we do?" I asked, wiping my brow and taking a long drink from my water bottle. I drank with such abandon that water trickled down my chin and onto my shirt.

"Not good enough," Harold confessed. His own brow was dripping wet, his shirt and pants and everything else, too.

"What do you mean?" I asked.

"Well," he hesitated, as though about to deliver bad news. "We did just under 2,600 feet."

"Oh," I said, my water bottle suspended in mid-air. Doing some quick calculations of my own, I decided against asking how my ordinarily infallible planner could have gotten it so wrong.

"Thank god it's early," he commented, after unwrapping a protein bar and taking a bite.

"Why's that?" I asked, happy he'd found a silver lining.

"Because we still have enough time to do it again."

I nearly spit out my water—but I didn't protest.

Instead, I followed Harold all the way back down to sea level—to a different beach than where we started, to keep things interesting—turned around, and hiked all the way up the mountain a second time. After a short rest, we did yet another U-turn and returned to where our adventure had begun what now seemed a lifetime ago.

We were on the trails almost twelve hours that day. Ironically, that got us within reach of the expected duration of the Mount Whitney ascent, estimated to take between twelve and eighteen hours.

Although at the time his surprise seemed sincere, in hindsight I have no doubt Harold knew all along that one climb was not going to suffice. He researched everything,

## I Will Be the Woman He Loved

and had to have been perfectly aware of Mt. Tam's elevation. He probably just figured it would be easier to get me to go along with a second trip if it appeared an unfortunate, unforeseen necessity.

After our double dose of Mt. Tam, our training continued, including many hikes on 4,342-foot Mount Saint Helena, visible from our Sonoma County bedroom. We climbed other nearby mountains, too—though none of them allowed us to start from sea level, denying us the novelty of our first expedition.

In the end, all the preparation paid off. We did in fact make it to the top of Mount Whitney, an unforgettable, one-in-a-lifetime experience we shared with our friend Bob, my brother, our cousin Nenad from Croatia, and Yves, a French friend who had trekked with us in the Himalayas years before.

Harold always knew what he had to do.

I was always happy to join him.

---

Realizing that our very different approaches nonetheless allowed us to reach the same goals, something clicks.

How I traveled with Harold is how I move forward on my own. There's no clearly defined goal guiding me down a well-planned path. I'm finding my way through my grief and beyond my loss as I go, wandering through uncharted territory, following my curiosity and trusting it will always lead to something worthwhile, spectacular or mundane.

Returning my attention to the trail, I noticed for the first time that I was running out of daylight. Whereas until now I had cherished my solitude, looking down the isolated stretch of river edged with dense shrubbery and trees, I suddenly felt alone—and uneasy. Overhanging branches that would normally inspire instead harbored cold and darkness, while narrow trails vanished into the thick undergrowth. Instead of leading to bucolic, dusky meadows, in my mind's eye they concealed stalkers awaiting unsuspecting victims.

I sped up. I walk more than three miles an hour, and this jaunt was supposed to be less than six miles. Since I left at 3:30 in the afternoon, at the latest I would get to the town by 5:30. Surely, I thought, even in an English winter the sun wouldn't set before that. Or would it?

I decided to jog for a bit, reminding myself I had run a half marathon in a not-too-distant past. As my pulse quickened, my temperature rose. First my gloves came off. Then my hat. It wasn't long before my jacket was too much, so I tied it around my waist. I hit my stride, but the sun didn't slow its descent. The lower it fell, the more anxious I became.

Then I heard a shout.

My heart jumped. I stopped.

Looking around—my eyes darting here, then there—I couldn't tell where the shout came from. I listened for another. I just wanted to get to the damned town. How much farther could it be?

I waited a few moments without hearing anything else. Convinced I wasn't under any sort of imminent threat, I resumed my jog, again picking up my pace.

Around the next bend, the river filled with boats and rowers. An enthusiastic rowing coach shouted at his team.

I should have recognized that sound by now.

I approached a boarding school and stopped some

young boys, who—much to my relief—confirmed I was approaching my destination.

Just as the sun set, an arched brick bridge enshrouded by the tragic, elegant boughs of a few weeping willows appeared, a line of traffic on both ends. Beyond it, on the opposite bank, at long last I saw my destination, the Great House Hotel.

Another traditional half-timbered style building, it also had the familiar terracotta tile roof, bay windows with white wooden frames, and a few chimneys. Inside was just as familiar and charming, though at the moment I was little concerned with the details. Instead, I checked in and headed straight for my room.

No sooner had I dropped my things and fallen onto the bed than the phone rang.

"Oh good," said Linda. "You're here! I just got back, and I found something I need to show you."

After a quick shower, I met Linda downstairs. A grin on her face, she didn't say a word as she led me to a churchyard across the road. She followed a path around the church, its walls dappled gray stone, its roof a surprising, vibrant orange-red, and into a small graveyard. Modest, unadorned tombstones appeared to be made of the same stone as the church, though a dusting of moss had turned many of them green. Given her determined clip, clearly Linda's feet were no longer bothering her.

"Where are you taking me?" I demanded, doing my best to keep up.

"You'll see!" was all I got in return.

As night continued to fall, we emerged from the tombstones and onto a circular driveway. I should have known: she had brought me to a pub.

Over the course of our days on the trail, Linda had become a pub aficionada. She could recognize a good one a mile away. The building housing this particular pub, The Bull, was owned by the church whose cemetery we had just traversed. Immaculate white brick with exposed wood beams painted black and leaded-glass windows, here both body and soul could be nourished.

We stepped inside, greeted by the sounds of conversation and glass clinking glass. I snagged a spot for us by the fire, while Linda went to the bar. The place was filling up.

As I waited, I took in the surroundings. Wood beams in the walls and low-hanging ceiling were the same black we'd seen on the façade. I chuckled when overhead I saw that some featured quotes in praise of ale, including "For a quart of ale is a dish for a king," from Shakespeare's *The Winter's Tale*. The floors, too, were wood, while some of the walls were plastered, others white brick, again like the façade. When I'd glanced in the dining room on the way in, I spied two old revolvers hung on plaques over a large fireplace, which had been turned into a wine rack, under lock and key. Dog treats in a glass jar on a windowsill were more freely available to any deserving pooch.

"The bartender says the building was built in the 1600s!" Linda shared, as she handed me a mojito. Excited to indulge in our end-of-day ritual, I took a sip.

"That good, huh?" Linda said facetiously, seeing my expression.

"Let's just say we've had better."

She took a drink.

"Oh god, you're right," she agreed, smacking her lips. "Something is very off!"

"Maybe the rum's been around since the 1600s, too!"

I laughed, having another drink, while trying to ignore the taste.

No matter. We were so happy to be here, they could have served us wine turned to vinegar, and we wouldn't have minded.

Two couples in their forties sat down next to us. All locals and observing that we weren't, they asked where we were from. Soon we were telling them about our walk. When our stomachs begin to stir, we asked them for food recommendations. We ordered, then continued chatting. Not long after our meals arrived.

"This pub is so cute," I said to one of the women, after she turned down my offer of some fries—or *chips* as they were called here.

"It's one of our favorites," she agreed, gesturing to her partner, a handsome fellow who was now conversing with their other friends. "And it's actually quite well known—it was even in *Three Men in a Boat*."

"You mean the book?" I asked, recalling the earlier mention. The pub had gotten louder. I felt as though I were practically yelling at her.

"Yeah," she said, "And the Clooneys have shown up from time to time."

"Clooneys?" Linda interjected. "You mean, like George Clooney?"

"Yeah, he and his wife Amal bought the mill not far from here."

"I was already thinking this might be my favorite pub so far," Linda said, "And now I'm sure of it!"

"Just keep your eye on the door," I laughed, "Maybe we'll get lucky!"

# Condition of Entry

"Downton Abbey was filmed near here," the young hostess told us the next morning at breakfast, "So we're expecting many more visitors from the US."

Dressed in more formal attire than we'd seen elsewhere, vaguely recalling the post-Edwardian period in which the television series took place, this thirtysomething with short, wavy brown hair might have just walked off a soundstage.

As for the setting of the current scene, we found ourselves in a spacious dining room featuring clean lines and bold colors. Booths, including the one we were sitting in, were a bright avocado. The walls and doors were ocean blue, as was the long, highbacked bench that bisected the room, simple wooden tables and chairs lining the length of it. Three brick columns broke up the wall of the bar, shelves between them stocked with bottles of wine and glasses hung upside down, as though unfairly punished. At the far end of the room two sofas faced each other, welcoming guests to sit in front of a fireplace where, at the moment, no wood was crackling, no flames flickering.

"Really?" I said, surprised by yet another interesting bit of trivia. "Can we walk there from here? Is it on the way to Henley?"

George had failed to materialize the night before. Perhaps we could see Downton Abbey instead.

"Oh, no," she replied. "Highclere Castle is about thirty

miles away. We'll be running coaches."

"Well, I guess we won't have time for Downton Abbey," Linda said, turning back to the hostess. "We're walking the Thames Path from Oxford, and today we're going to Henley."

"Oh, you're doing the Thames Path," the young woman said. "That's great! We don't get many Americans walking around here. Most of them come in cars, you know. They love their cars, they do, the Americans."

We couldn't deny it.

"My boyfriend has done parts of the path," she continued, "but I've never walked all the way to Henley. Isn't it cold, doing it in winter? Most people come in summer."

We told our story yet again, hoping to expand her notion of Americans to allow for the possibility that there were at least a few walkers among us.

"Tell your friends to come visit Downton Abbey," she repeated, when the time came for us to leave. "They can take a comfortable coach, and we'll serve afternoon tea—just like they do in the series. I think it will be nicer than walking. Especially in winter."

Lucky for us, as Linda and I set off for Henley, the sun was out and the weather was unseasonably warm. The hotel's vine-covered hedge ushered us a short distance to a one-lane bridge, where a traffic light controlled an alternating flow of cars.

"How much breakfast did you eat?" I asked Linda, while we waited for a break in the traffic, so we could cross the street.

"What do you mean?" she balked, looking at her stomach. "You saw—I had a normal breakfast!"

"So you don't feel particularly heavy?"

"Heavy?" she countered, increasingly bewildered. "Tania, what are you talking about!"

"Well I just wanted to be sure—because apparently the bridge is weak!"

I pointed to a sign at the foot of it, which said, quite simply, "Weak Bridge."

We burst into laughter.

"Well, yeah, I guess if I had known I would have eaten a little less," Linda added, before—taking a risk we never would have suspected—we crossed the bridge, its walls made of brick seemingly at the limits of its load-bearing weight. Thankfully, along with the considerably heavier cars crossing alongside us, we made it to the other side without incident. There we crossed a second bridge, this one for pedestrians only, which took us over a tributary and back onto the riverside trail.

As we passed willows weeping leafless tears and pastures whose once-white fences had long since fallen victim to the elements, the trail now mere inches from the water, I recalled that Sue and John had called Henley a high point of their trip. The Royal Regatta, one of the oldest and most prestigious rowing competitions, is held there every July. A highlight of the so-called British "social season," it is executed with great fanfare and strict, high-society dress codes.

During my online research the night before, I learned not only that the regatta is visited by more than 300,000 people each year and that it includes more than 300 races over six days, but something very unexpected about its history.

Starting in 1886, the competition barred anyone from competing who had ever performed manual labor. In 1920 this led to the exclusion of John B. Kelly, Sr., an American who had done an apprenticeship as a bricklayer. Long since a successful businessman, he also happened to be a three-time Olympic rowing champion. No matter. Having laid a few bricks, he wasn't allowed to compete at Henley.

Assuming he was around to see it, Kelly, Sr. likely got no small amount of satisfaction years later when his son, John B. Kelly, Jr., won the 1947 Diamond Sculls at Henley.

Another interesting fact: Kelly, Sr.'s daughter was none other than Grace Kelly, the Academy Award-winning actress who went on to become Princess of Monaco. I couldn't help but think that the regatta never again shamed Kelly, Sr. for any perceived lack of social standing. Then again, he had probably wasted no time turning his attention from a club on the Thames to a palace on the Mediterranean.

The walk from Sonning to Henley took a little more than two hours. The trail meandered through flat expanses of fenced pastures bordered by trees. Occasionally there were small islands in the middle of the river. At others, big houseboats, long and low, were moored to the shore.

When we eventually reached the Shiplake lock, a few covered rowboats tied up along its concrete waterfront, the trail left behind the river, merging with a narrow, tree-lined road. Most of the rest of the day's walk would be spent in and out of neighborhoods, homes and apartments peering at us from behind hedges.

Somewhere between Sonning and Henley, Linda and I started talking about our respective children. When Harold and I were first married Linda met both our kids, preteens at the time. She could hardly believe they both now had offspring of their own.

"I remember what a tough teenager Brad always was," she said. "How does he like being a father?"

"It's really incredible. Brad is a wonderful father, an equal partner in raising the kids. I think the concept of being an absent dad—working long hours at the office while the kids grow up without him around—is antithetical to everything he believes in. Unlike his own dad must've been, he's no stranger to diapers!" I laughed.

"I feel so happy that Brad and Beth and their kids are so present in my life," I continued. "I never wanted my own, and it's such a gift to have two who showed up with the baby years behind them. Luckily, Harold and Lucy had an amicable divorce, so she didn't poison them against me. She came to the funeral, you know. I really like her, and think she's a great mother. We've had our challenges, but we've all stayed close."

"It's amazing," Linda mused. "Sometimes I wonder what happened to all that rebelliousness our generation exhibited when we were young."

"Oh my god! When I was sixteen there was no way you'd get me on a trip with my parents! I would have been mortified to even be seen with them! On the other hand, when I was a kid we vacationed in converted chicken coops on the Stanislaus River!" I recalled, laughing. "It was a far cry from places like Italy and Cancún, where we took Brad and Beth!"

As we talked, we came upon a small railroad track winding through a large, manicured garden. The tracks crossed little bridges, climbed up small hills, and passed a whole village of miniature homes, all big enough for small children.

We called over the gardener. An older fellow with the fit body, dirty nails, and leathery skin of someone who has spent decades under the sun, soon he was regaling us with stories about the eccentric owner and his friends.

"The kids must have so much fun on the train," I remarked.

"Kids?" he retorted. "M'am, that train is for the adults!"

We all laughed, at least one of us secretly hoping we were about to be offered a ride. Sadly, the gardener didn't go that far. We enjoyed our chat all the same.

As we moved on, the trail rounded a bend, approached the river, and ushered us into Henley. As it did, a large glass and wood structure with a pitched roof appeared on our left. A row of parking spaces in front, it looked as though it might have been a refurbished barn. As we came upon the entrance, we discovered it was the River and Rowing Museum.

Officially opened in November 1998 by Queen Elizabeth, the museum has permanent galleries featuring the River Thames, Henley itself, and the sport of rowing, from its early beginnings in ancient Greece all the way to the modern Olympics. In 2004, a permanent *The Wind in the Willows* exhibition was added, where 3D models depict the celebrated adventures of Mr. Toad, Ratty, Badger, and Mole.

Kindly asking Mr. Toad for a raincheck, we left behind the museum and continued into the town proper, where we weren't surprised to discover that all was quiet. We easily found our way to the Phyllis Court Club.

Presiding over a broad, straight stretch of river near the town's main bridge, it consisted of a white, two-story mansion with a large wing—the windowed Orangery—that served as the breakfast room.

"Uh, this looks fancy," Linda said, hesitating.

I looked at her, then down at my own dirty hiking attire. I got out my phone.

"Ha!" I burst out, "The hotel website has dress codes for every area of the club!"

"It does?" Linda said. "Every area?"

"Yes, look!"

I held up a chart detailing how club members were expected to dress. The Members Bar and Lounge Orangery had the same requirements, but they varied depending on the time of day. Before 6:30 casual and "smart casual" were acceptable; after 6:30, only smart casual was permitted. The chart explained that included slacks; jeans that were not faded, torn, or ripped; collared shirts or turtlenecks; and nice footwear. "Ladies" were expected to dress to a similar standard—presumably the main description was for men? Smart casual did *not* include any of the following: shorts, sweatsuits, trainers, flip flops, or open-toed sandals for gentlemen. It was unclear whether "ladies" could wear them.

For anyone dining in the Thames Room at any time, smart casual with a jacket was de rigueur. Codes were even specified for the terrace and lawn, even if, thankfully, casual dress was permitted for both. Club functions had their own specific codes, and for the regatta not only was there a code, but adherence to it was "a condition of entry."

"Phyllis Court staff are aware of the Code and will approach any member who they feel is not meeting the required standards," Linda read, once she'd made her way to the bottom of the chart.

"Hopefully they won't kick us out!" I joked.

"Well, they have to let us in first!" Linda retorted.

We headed up from the riverside to the club, going around to the front, since no doors facing the river were open. As we approached the entrance, we discovered that the dress code was posted there. Linda and I looked at each other, suppressing a laugh—even though, clearly, here attire was no laughing matter.

We walked inside, where we spied a discrete reception that almost seemed intentionally hidden from view, as though the hotel didn't want members to know that non-members could stay the night. On the wall behind the reception, yet another sign reminded visitors of the strictly enforced dress code.

"Oh my god," Linda muttered under her breath.

Thankfully, this sign was most concerned with ratty jeans and bare feet. Our own feet were covered, and our hiking pants—though admittedly layered in the same mud as our shoes—were not ratty denim. All the same, our prospects weren't looking good.

"Welcome!" said the man and woman behind the reception desk. Immaculately dressed and coiffed, with perfect complexions and the brightest of smiles, they were the very image of youthful decorum.

Linda and I let out a sigh of relief, as well as another laugh. Here, like everywhere thus far on the trail, we were to receive a warm welcome. Even at someplace with as many rules as the Phyllis Court Club, concessions were made for through hikers.

The two staff explained that, although the bar normally had a stricter evening dress code than the lobby, we were welcome to eat there. Still, as we looked around at the other code-adhering guests, Linda and I decided we'd be more comfortable dining elsewhere.

We had lunch at a casual restaurant nearby. Linda then returned to her room to relax and soak her feet, while I slipped out to wander around town.

Leaving through the back of the hotel, I followed a narrow lane past old, two-story houses painted white. At the end of the lane, the Thames reappeared to my left, forcing a busy street into a tight turn. Walking away from the river, I continued past a succession of tasteful two- and three-story red-brick homes with white trim. Not a tree lined the handsome lane, though here and there greenery clung to façades and gates. The sidewalks were paved in flagstones.

I passed a hotel and a beer bottler—though I suspected the sign was a historic one—a dry cleaner and a theater. Taking a left, I found myself on a still more commercial street, starting with a toy shop and a Domino's Pizza. A hairdresser and a restaurant were followed by a café and a succession of cute boutiques. Clearly this single lane was the center of town. I took my time exploring and peering into windows, before eventually retracing my steps and heading back to the hotel.

Late in the afternoon, Sharon returned from her night in London. Once she was settled in her room, the three of us wandered back out for a stroll, which, as night began to fall, became a search for a place to have a drink.

The darker it got, the more the streets emptied and the livelier the pubs became. We passed a few, struggling to settle on one—they all looked so fun and inviting. By the time we picked our favorite, The Angel—right on the bridge—it was full. Tired of walking and emboldened by our thirst, we decided to squeeze our way inside.

In some ways another quintessentially English pub,

wood beams overhead and a fireplace keeping things warm, here the colors were lighter and brighter than some of the other locales we'd visited. The floors were yellow pine. The walls had robin-egg blue wainscotting, white above; one of them featured a vibrant floral wallpaper. The furniture was a fun, eclectic mix of mismatched tables and chairs.

Midway through our first round, the bartender let us know a table in back had freed up. We made a beeline for it, getting there at the same time as two young British women. An awkward standoff ensued: all of us lunged at the table, shamelessly hellbent on staking our claim; then, catching ourselves, we regained not only our composure but our manners, each group offering the table to the other. We went back and forth a couple of times before it finally occurred to us: the table was big enough. We could sit together.

More drinks were ordered, and soon we were chatting up a storm. Both women were in their twenties. Dressed for a night out on the town, long, shiny hair coiffed, make-up meticulously applied, they were fit, attractive, and self-possessed. Laura's family had been British for as long as they could remember; Adriana's grandparents had moved to England from Italy. Both Laura and Adriana found Henley stuffy and boring but chose to live here because of their well-paying jobs.

"And where are you ladies staying?" Laura asked, turning the focus on us.

"At the Phyllis Court Club," I replied.

Laura and Adriana almost choked on their drinks, shooting each other looks I couldn't let go unnoticed.

"What!" I demanded, "You don't like it?"

"*Like* it!" Adriana balked, a flash in her dark eyes, "As

if we've ever stepped inside!"

"Oh my god, the Phyllis Court Club is the absolute stuffiest of all the stuffy places in town!" Laura declared, as though it were inconceivable we hadn't figured that out on our own.

"It's the supreme pinnacle of stuffiness," Adriana agreed, taking another drink, no doubt to cope with the cluelessness of the naïve old Americans.

"Not only have we never been," Laura added, now on a roll, "but—until this very moment—I doubt we've even actually spoken to anyone who has!"

"Not like they'd talk to *us*!" Adriana added with a smirk.

"Well," Linda admitted, "they certainly do have a strict dress code!"

The conversation veered off in two directions, Linda and Sharon talking with Laura, and I conversing with Adriana. Her immigrant grandparents had retired in their northern Italian hometown, and her grandfather was now writing a series of three novels about their family. The first began 500 years ago in the Middle East, as infidel armies clashed with a group of Christians who eventually become Adriana's ancestors.

I shared that I was considering writing a similar history and that my family emigrated 500 years ago from Montenegro to what was then part of the Venetian empire. They fled the Turks who were decimating the local populations, distant precursors to the contemporary battles of Kosovo. Although my family was Slav, they lived very close to where Adriana's Italian ancestors lived. I didn't mention that it was her ancestors who forced my mother's family to flee. A story for another time.

"It's funny that your family ended up in America and mine in Britain," Adriana commented, "and now we just happen to have come together in a bar."

"Because there were no empty tables!" I added, as we both laughed.

We older ladies bought everyone another round of drinks, as well as so many snacks we ended up having no need of dinner. Instead, we continued chatting with our lovely new friends, who kept us out well past what ordinarily would have been our bedtime.

# A New Woman

We left Henley Thursday morning under cloudy skies. Clouds or no clouds, though, we still hadn't seen rain since Abingdon. It was getting warmer every day.

In and out of fields and forests, following the right bank of the river, we passed the entire course of the Henley Regatta on our way toward Marlow, where Sharon and I would get a ride to Cliveden.

Cliveden is an enormous, well-known manor on 350 acres rising from the Thames. A good day's walk beyond Henley, it was once home to the Duke of Windsor, before the Astor family purchased it in the early twentieth century. When they decided to move on, they donated the property to the National Trust. It's now a hotel with more than forty rooms. Until Sharon surprised me with reservations—something she sprung on me midway down the trail—I wasn't even aware it was possible to stay there. I was, however, aware of Cliveden's fame—and infamy.

In 1961, Lord Astor invited a group that included Secretary of State for War, John Profumo, to Cliveden for the weekend. Poolside, Profumo met nineteen-year old model Christine Keeler, with whom he began an extramarital affair. When news of the affair broke in 1963—made worse by rumors that Keeler was also the mistress of an alleged Soviet spy—Profumo denied it in the House of Commons. Weeks later a police investigation exposed the truth, damaging not only Profumo's reputation but the credibility of then Prime Minister Harold Macmillan's government. Macmillan was forced to resign, and the Conservative government was defeated by the Labour Party in the 1964 general election.

Although the most notorious, I couldn't help but assume the Profumo affair was just one of many such stories Cliveden's walls would tell if only they could talk. Perhaps, if we were lucky, Sharon and I would be involved in our own history-making scandal there. Hard to imagine, though, that we'd have any luck bringing down a government.

If we did, it would be without Linda's help. She planned to walk with us only as far as a village called Hurley, where she would get a taxi to Marlow. She was meeting her daughter at London's Waterloo train station at 2:30. Although excited about seeing her, she was also sad to be ending our adventure.

We all were, suddenly overcome by the realization of how much we had enjoyed each other's company and how good the walk had been for each of us.

Linda had come a long way in a few short days. Smiling much of the time, the Linda who walked with us now had more of the bounce and enthusiasm of the Linda I knew in Minneapolis. She had gotten clarity on her relationship, realized she wasn't "boring," and reclaimed her power. As our time together came to an end, she exuded a confidence and focus lacking at the beginning of our trip.

"My resolve hasn't wavered," she explained, as we walked. "My relationship with Bruce is over. I honestly feel free of him and any pull he had on me. I see it all so clearly now—there's no looking back. And it's because of this time together."

"What do you think you'll do when you get home?"

Sharon asked.

"For starters, I'm going back to Minnesota, finalize my divorce, and put Bruce out of my mind! And I'm not going to get a full-time job. Life is short. There's too many things I still want to do with mine."

The trail veered away from the river, rambling through an enormous seventeenth century estate. We met the project manager, a tall, trim forty-something with slicked-back hair, a prominent nose, and what—to my untrained ear at least—sounded like an aristocratic accent. Graciously pausing for a moment from his work, he explained that the manor façade had just been renovated to exacting specifications and that the grounds were being restored, as well. In an unexpected twist, he also divulged that the property was owned by the same Swiss investment banker who owned the estate with the model train. Looking around, I was disappointed not to see any tracks.

We had heard about this massive restoration project from some people in Henley. They expressed misgivings about a foreigner owning such a major swath of British countryside.

I thought of Cliveden, so quintessentially British, but owned by the American Astor. Britain had solved that problem by making him a lord, conferring upon him much desired social status and proving beneficial to the country, as well, between the resources he invested and his eventual bequest of much of his estate to the National Trust.

If the monarchy and class system in Britain retain any value beyond encouraging tourism, surely it must be in attracting financial resources of global elite looking to attain conspicuous social status. Perhaps this Swiss gentleman would follow in Astor's footsteps, and we would soon be reading about his own knighthood.

As reality continued to sink in and Sharon, Linda, and I became increasingly aware of our time together drawing to an end, we found ourselves taking more and more photos, something easy to do here. From the gently rolling lawns to the lush groves of trees to the tranquil pond, the grounds were full of picturesque spots. We took full advantage of them.

---

A few hours later a weir appeared—a low-head dam, over which water cascades to a lower level in a river or other body of water—given away by a long concrete-and-metal footbridge on top of it. An abrupt, tree-covered hillside served as picturesque backdrop. At the same time, an island appeared, followed by two more. Passing a weathered houseboat moored to the shore, we then came upon a tall, arching footbridge that would have taken us to still another island. Instead, we took a right and arrived in Hurley.

A path meandered past a church, then a two-story red-brick bed and breakfast. We walked by other homes and buildings—but were surprised to find that nothing was open. No one was in the streets. After wandering around a little more but having no luck, we searched for a pub on Google Maps. The Olde Bell came up. We headed in its direction.

The pub turned out be another historic timber-frame building with a steeply pitched, shingle-covered roof. True to its name, a sign with an old bell hung over the entrance. Walls painted white, exposed timbers painted black, multi-paned windows of leaded glass, it also conveyed a contemporary sophistication.

Pushing on its heavy door, we walked into a large room devoid of guests, welcomed instead by a crackling fire. Not a moment to lose, Linda freed her sore feet from the binding imprisonment of her shoes and plopped into a high-backed easy chair facing the flames.

Without bothering to ask Linda what she wanted to drink, Sharon and I approached the bar, its carved wood stained dark. Two stools in front of it awaited guests. They didn't have to ask twice.

"Hello?" I called out, instinctively looking for a bell.

Nothing.

"Hello!" I hollered again.

A door closed. We heard footsteps.

"Coming!" replied a male voice.

A handsome, middle-aged man appeared, his otherwise dark hair gray at the temples. Before we had given it any thought, he offered us beers. We accepted.

"So, why the 'Olde Bell'?" I couldn't help but ask.

"Well, when it first opened in 1135, the Olde Bell was—"

"Eleven thirty what?" I interrupted.

He handed us our glasses of beer, foam on each threatening to jump overboard. Sharon and I took a drink. Linda's lay untouched on the counter.

"1135," he said. "The inn is nearly 850 years old."

I about spit out the brew.

"850 years!" I cried out.

"Linda, did you hear that? The inn is 850 years old!" I exclaimed.

"Yeah, I heard! Incredible!" she called back, not budging from the comfort of her fireside seat. Sharon kindly got up and delivered her beer.

"As I was saying," the bartender continued, "when it first opened, it was a guest house for visitors to the Benedictine priory. They had a bell they rang to let the monks know that a visitor had arrived in the village and was on their way."

"I love it!" I exclaimed, taking another drink and looking around the bar, struggling to believe it could really be that old. Black and white photos hung here and there, along with large, antique keys, which offered no clue as to what mysteries they might unlock. White walls took on a yellow hue in the dim light, as did painted beams overhead. Red ceramic tiles underfoot covered the floors.

"A revolution was plotted here. Winston Churchill and Dwight D. Eisenhower stayed here during World War II. And Pinewood is nearby, so lots of Hollywood actors have stayed here."

"Pinewood?" asked Sharon.

"Pinewood Studios," he clarified. "Where they make *James Bond*—and lots of other movies. They made one of the *Alien* movies there. And a *Batman* one. Like I said, lots of them."

"Wow," said Sharon, wiping some foam from her lip.

"So, what stars have been here?" I had to know.

"Elizabeth Taylor. Richard Burton. Cary Grant. Errol Flynn. And more recently—at least compared to those stars—Dustin Hoffman."

"Too funny!" I said. "We had no idea! We just found you on Google Maps!"

While we'd been talking, locals had begun to trickle in, including the owners. Since we weren't exactly being discreet and had snagged prime real estate at the bar, gradually we were surrounded. Everyone was friendly, many ordering "the usual," while others were served their libation of choice without so much as a word.

The longer we spent with the warm, welcoming group—people coming, going, lingering to chat—the more we began to feel part of the town's extended family.

When we realized how hungry we were, the bartender asked if we wanted to dine in the restaurant or eat in the bar. We looked over at Linda. She wasn't going anywhere—and neither were we.

We ordered a ploughman's lunch and a scotch egg with apple sauce. I was oblivious to the origins of either name or what exactly they meant, but it didn't matter. What showed up was an egg with a runny yolk covered by sausage, as well as a delicious assortment of cheeses and pickled vegetables. We couldn't get enough of them.

When word got out that this was Linda's last day on the trail, the spontaneous festivities turned into an impromptu going-away party. Other than Sharon and I, no one had known her for more than an hour. It made no difference. Everyone was sorry she had to go.

"You can't be leaving already!" exclaimed a man at the bar.

"A week's not nearly enough!" cried a woman within earshot.

"But you've only just got here!" protested another man, as though doubting what he had heard.

As the hour of her departure approached, amidst the fun and games we had to consider some logistics. The innkeeper organized Linda's ride. He also informed us that her plan to catch a train in Marlow was flawed; better from nearby Maidenhead, where there was regular service to

Paddington Station. Linda nodded and thanked the innkeeper. But she was only half-listening.

She didn't seem to have any intention to leave.

The closer the time got for Linda to catch her taxi, the more Sharon and I checked our watches. Linda didn't notice. She was too busy eating, drinking, and having a good time.

Noon came and went. 12:30, too.

Sharon and I exchanged confused looks.

We all shared a dessert and had some tea. More people wandered in to warm up by the fire. The taxi arrived and parked just outside the door. No one seemed concerned.

Far from it. By now Linda had removed not only her shoes but her warm clothes. She had even shed her inhibitions.

As though she were a local, Linda rambled and laughed, boisterous and unabashed. Sharon and I looked at each other, our eyebrows raised. Who was this woman? She told jokes, she shared anecdotes, she reveled in being the center of attention, hogging the limelight. She may not have been a local, but the locals loved it—they loved her. They egged her on, begging for more, hanging onto her every word. Sharon and I did, too, barely recognizing this exuberant woman who seemed so different from the one who had accompanied us for days on the trail.

"And Bruce thought she was boring!" I quipped, elbowing Sharon.

We hated to interrupt. So we didn't. Linda's daughter could wait—and she'd be glad she did. We were sending her a renewed, reenergized version of her mother!

Linda finally came to her senses, looking at the clock with a start and realizing it was time to go. Past time, in fact. We exchanged quick hugs, while—still barefoot—she ran out of the pub, piled her stuff into the car, and headed off with a wave out the taxi window.

Sharon and I were also reluctant to leave this delightful spot and our new friends, but our time to go soon came as well. Our intention, after all, had simply been to find a place to eat! Clearly we had gotten much more out of the experience. All the same, there were many hours left in the day, and our destination remained: Cliveden. We were looking forward to spending our last night together there.

---

Back on the trail, Sharon told me she was more convinced than ever that she wanted to move beyond business and explore a new way of living. She wanted to continue traveling. She wanted to keep exploring art, to have more time to share experiences with friends. At the same time, she needed a new anchor to give her life the structure that her work always had.

Meanwhile, I floated in the island that was our experience on the trail, enjoying the present. I felt good, for the most part untroubled by the grief and sense of loss that had come and gone over the course of my time with my two friends.

That did not mean, however, that Harold did not continue to be ever present.

Like earlier with the cygnets, several times a day something would prompt me to think "Harold would love that!" Then I would remember he was no longer with me, that I couldn't call him or tell him about it. My body tensing, my stomach twisting, anguish would descend. Almost as soon as it did, anger followed. I was not going to wallow.

And so the sorrow didn't linger. Instead, it was like the seagulls at the beach in San Francisco. They face stiff breezes head on, holding steadily in place, as if deciding whether to push forward. Then they give in, letting go of their resistance and allowing themselves to be carried away by the wind. Like the gulls, I couldn't overcome the surges of my despair by fighting them head on. I had to let them flow through me. I had to continue giving into my desire to experience each new moment, allow that to help keep me aloft and moving forward.

As the river curved around a large bend, the sky turned from overcast gray to a deep blue dappled with billowing white clouds. Sunlight danced on the water, and the river widened. The path transitioned into a bright green lawn along the riverbank, where a jumble of children, dogs, and parents played in the sunshine. More movie-set swans floated majestically on the river, and a bridge appeared in the distance.

We had reached Marlow. As we approached the bridge, we saw that it was a suspension one, a large stone arch on each end. Its cables and wooden lattice railings glowed white in the sun. Built in the early 1800s, use of the bridge was now limited to foot traffic and local driving. A 2016 incident with a thirty-seven-ton Lithuanian truck hadn't caused any damage, but it did result in a two-month closure of the bridge. No one wanted a repeat of that mishap.

Across the river, some tables were set up on an expansive lawn. A couple walked out to the tables, followed moments later by a waiter who brought a tea service.

"What is that beautiful building?" I asked.

I gestured to a conjoined succession of two- and three-story brick buildings with white shutters, an atrium on one end, and what might have been a converted barn on the other, both painted immaculate white. Like the nearby bridge, the sprawling structure was radiant. As though out of deference, the river widened yet again before it.

"That's the Compleat Angler!" said Sharon. "I forgot it was even here!"

The only Compleat Angler I knew was in one of my favorite books, the best-selling novel *The River Why*, by David James Duncan. *The Compleat Angler* served as the most revered book in the protagonist's childhood home, his parents quoting and misquoting it when discussing artificial flies.

I didn't know it at the time, but *The Compleat Angler* was a real book, written by the seventeenth-century English author Izaak Walton. A prose and verse celebration of fishing, it was first published in 1653, though Walton continued to expand it over the course of the twenty-five years that followed. By the time the last edition was published, the original thirteen chapters had grown to twenty-one, a second part added by Walton's friend Charles Cotton. Cotton picked up the protagonist's story where Walton left off, completing his instruction in fly fishing and the making of flies.

More concerned with getting a closer look at the marvelous hotel than reflecting on its ties to literature, Sharon and I headed to the bridge and crossed the river.

Scarcely had we set foot on its grounds, than I developed a major case of hotel envy. I didn't merely want to have tea on its lawn, like the couple still enjoying their own service; I wanted to stay here. I wanted to indulge in the sun, the warmth, the vibrance of this magical place.

Sharon and I looked at each other. We were sharing the same secret longing. But Cliveden was already booked.

"Cliveden will be just as nice," I said.

"Of course," Sharon replied, as though trying to convince herself she believed it.

"But we can at least have tea here," I suggested.

"Absolutely. Then, you know, we can continue to Cliveden."

"Right."

We walked across the lawn toward the lucky couple, who were sitting at the only table with a white tablecloth. As we wiped water from the seats of a neighboring table and sat down, the enticing aroma of a fresh Earl Grey tea wafted our way, carried by a breeze off the river.

"That looks lovely," I said to them, nearly blinded by the glint of silver.

The couple was younger than they'd seemed from a distance, probably in their mid-thirties. Tall, bespectacled, his light hair thinning on top, he wore a zipped-up, dark-blue jacket, pressed slacks, and polished loafers. Her dyed blond locks pulled into a neat ponytail, the petite woman wore a bright-red coat, from under which a skirt draped to her knees.

"It is! We can't believe we're having it outside in February! We live nearby, and this is our first time outside in months—it's been so cold," the man explained, as he poured the young woman another cup of tea.

"You look like you walked," she added, steam rising from her cup. "What a lucky day you chose!"

"We can hardly believe it ourselves!" I replied. After looking over my shoulder, I asked, "Will a waiter come take our order?"

"I'm afraid not," the woman said. "They don't serve out here in mid-winter."

"Go to the front desk and ask for Gordon," the man advised. "He might bring you some. We're regulars, which is why he brought us ours."

Sharon stayed behind while I went inside. A woman called Gordon, who laughed and said that, of course, he would bring us tea. He seemed happy for the distraction. The place was nearly abandoned. The staff must have been bored.

I headed back outside. Gordon followed shortly after with the requisite white tablecloth and napkins. He took our order and disappeared.

He'd only been gone a minute when Sharon's phone rang. Before I heard a single word, I knew: Cliveden.

"Hold on just a moment please," she said into the phone.

"It's Cliveden," she confirmed, turning to me. "They have a burst water main. We can still stay in our rooms, but we won't be able to shower, and they won't be able to serve us dinner. What do you want to do?"

"Tell them we'll call right back!" I whispered.

I didn't want to jinx the fortuitous turn of events. What were the chances! In all my traveling I had never had a hotel cancel a room—and certainly not at the exact moment I was seriously regretting having made a very expensive, nonrefundable reservation someplace I no longer wanted to stay.

Sharon hung up.

"Let's see if we can get a room here!" I said, practically giddy.

"Yes!"

Leaving our tea to steep on its own, we ran to the lobby. The staff happily offered us a deal on two riverfront rooms.

Back down by the river, Sharon called Cliveden and relieved them of their obligation to us. She hung up the phone and gave me a high five.

"We're free!" I exclaimed.

Amidst our celebration, Gordon showed up with a tray of scones. Before he left, we asked to reserve spots in the hotel's gourmet restaurant, which was also on the river.

After lingering a while over the tea, Sharon and I went to our rooms to clean up. Then we each headed out to wander around town on our own.

I found myself exploring the riverbank, where families were packing up and heading home, now that the sun had begun its slow descent. As it did, it fell behind a curtain of clouds, turning what had been the bridge's sparkling white into a subdued gray.

My eyes still on the bridge, I was reminded of a trip I took with Harold and my mom, Zora, before she, too, lost her radiance, making her own descent into dementia.

---

I was born in Belgrade, Yugoslavia. My mother, Croatian by birth, was displaced by Mussolini's takeover of Istria—a peninsula just below Trieste, Italy—after World War I. My father, a Russian, was displaced by the Communist revolution of 1917. Before I was a year old, all of us were displaced by a post-World War II feud between Tito and Stalin, the leaders of my two homelands. We spent years in a refugee camp in what is now Italy, eventually emigrating to the United States and settling in San Francisco.

In the early 1990s, after a period of political and economic crises, Yugoslavia cracked apart like an overripe pomegranate dropped on a rock, some pieces scattering, others hanging together by the thick pith encasing the seeds. Only after several brutal wars did the country split definitively into the seven smaller ones we know today.

In the process, my Croatian and Serbian cousins suddenly became enemies, and my six aunts found themselves separated into warring enclaves between which all communication was cut. My mother in San Francisco was the only link holding together their fractured world.

Meanwhile, the country of birth on my passport changed from Yugoslavia to Belgrade (was it now forbidden to even print the word *Serbia*?), to Serbia and Montenegro to, ultimately, Serbia. It seemed wrong. Even if held in contempt, shouldn't your place of birth remain an immutable absolute?

By the summer of 2000, the wars—first within the countries of the former Yugoslavia, then between Serbia and NATO over Kosovo—were finally over. Like the USSR, the evil Communist empire that preceded it, Serbia had gone down in flames of contempt, the new pariah of the Western world.

The end of the chaos meant we could take Mama back to Croatia, where three of her sisters lived, and to Serbia, to visit the other three.

Harold was looking forward to Croatia. He was excited to see Nenad again, my cousin who had climbed Mt. Whitney with us, and to meet the rest of my Croatian family.

He was less sure about Serbia. It didn't help that NATO had just bombed it. We and our allies had destroyed buildings, a radio tower in Belgrade, and bridges across the Danube. Thousands died. Serbia was unrepentant.

"They'll hate me for being American!" Harold fretted one morning while discussing the trip. The kitchen smelled of coffee.

"Oh no," my mother reassured him, oil sizzling as she fried a few thin strips of bacon, "you'll be with us. No one will even know you're American!"

He was 6'6". He didn't know a single word of Serbian. He was skeptical.

"You're family," Mama insisted, looking up from the skillet and seeing he wasn't convinced. "They'll love you. No one will even bring up the bombing."

We flew to Croatia, where we had a delightful time with family. Then we headed to Serbia.

When we pulled up to our hotel, Harold's jaw dropped. Mama and I pretended not to see the bombed-out TV tower across the street.

From Belgrade we continued to Novi Sad, where my aunt, six cousins, and more than fifty other family members lived. Some of them lived across the Danube River from Novi Sad, in the village of Petrovradin. All three bridges crossing the river had been bombed. Again, by us. One had been rebuilt on floating barrels. We used it to cross to the one-room house where my aunt raised six children who shared a single giant bed.

That same evening the clan gathered nearby, in my cousin's apartment: my aunt, the six siblings, their spouses, a few kids, my mother, Harold, and I. Though bigger than my aunt's house, the apartment was not large. I'm not sure how we all fit in the living room, but we managed. More of us than I would have thought possible squeezed onto the single sofa, the arms of the big chair served as perches, and a few more seats were brought in from the kitchen. The floor proved just as good a place to sit as any, as least for the youngest among us.

My eyes darting around the room as I found my own spot, I glimpsed old photos and a wooden clock on the wall, handmade doilies on the coffee table. I suspected the lace curtains over the windows, too, were the handiwork of my aunt.

Once we were settled, I introduced Harold to everyone. A traditional plum brandy, rakija, was served, and we started to chat. I served as interpreter.

"Why did you bomb our bridges?" my cousin Darko asked, right out of the gate. He was thin, with hair and eyes reminiscent of his name. Though he didn't miss a beat when asking the question, his tone wasn't accusatory. To the contrary, he was surprisingly warm, given what our country had just done to his. I couldn't help but think that if we could all approach difficult conversations like he did—directly but without aggression—we might peacefully resolve many more of the issues facing the world.

All that notwithstanding, I could hardly bear to translate his question, Harold's worst fears come true. As soon as I had, he shot me the look—the one that said, *I should have known better than to listen to you!* At the time it made me wince; now I'd give almost anything to see it again.

Harold took a deep breath as he formulated his response.

"You have thought about it a lot, I can tell," he began. "What do *you* think?"

The theories flowed. Some in the room believed the Americans were confused and had mistaken Novi Sad for Belgrade, a short distance away. Others thought it was payback for the nearby Srebrenica massacre, the July 1995 genocide of more than 8,000 Bosniak Muslims by units of a Bosnian Serb Army and a Serbian paramilitary unit. Other ideas were vigorously debated among the cousins, before Harold ventured that maybe NATO wanted to send a strong message without crippling the capital.

"In any case," he said, "I am so sorry my country has caused you so much harm."

Tough questions notwithstanding, apparently Harold passed the test that first night. The six brothers and husbands took him fishing and drinking. They all went to butcher the hog for cousin Stanko's neighbor. When he learned they had a shared interest in fossils, Radica took Harold to the university where he taught. For almost a week, Harold and the men were inseparable.

When the time came to return home, Harold knew that *riba* was fish, *pivo* was beer, and *hvala* was thank you. Far from being the despised American, he had been received as a beloved brother. He, in turn, had opened to the Serbs. What he had heard in the press not only painted them in the worst possible light, but it was also diametrically opposed to his newly acquired firsthand experience. Serbia was no longer a place to be feared or avoided; to the contrary, he looked forward to returning someday.

Reliving the memory made me teary. As I dabbed my eyes and came back to my senses, a shiver alerted me to how cold it had gotten. I left behind the bridge and headed inside to get ready for dinner.

All white, with a vaulted wood-beam ceiling and walls of glass doors on three sides, the dining room overlooked both the river and the bridge, once again aglow, now by a series of strategically placed lights. Sharon and I each decided on the prix fixe menu and wine.

Arguing and laughing our way through dinner, we continued an ongoing debate comparing life in the US and the UK. The current topic concerned the merits of a tutor-based education, as practiced at Oxford, compared with my crowded Berkeley classes, which had as many as 2000 students. I was serving on the advisory board there, Sharon was on one at Oxford. We went at it tooth and nail. I was proud of what at the time had been a very inexpensive education, and criticized what I perceived as the elitism of the British system.

Sharon cited a *New York Times* article that confirmed upward mobility had become greater in the United Kingdom than in the United States. Not familiar with the article, I couldn't speak to it; instead, I countered that the percentage of people who go on to a higher degree in the UK was still far lower than in the US.

"I'm not so sure," Sharon said. "Either way, at least it's only *you* I need to defend the UK against! Remember the debate we got into with Harold about the value of the monarchy at that *rifugio* in the Dolomites?"

No sooner had she mentioned the trip than she doubted herself, looking at me as though fearing she had overstepped, her glass suspended in midair. The trip, after all, had been one of the last good times Harold and I shared on the road. But I was fine, and soon Sharon and I were reminiscing.

Harold and I loved trekking through the Dolomites. When four of our Healdsburg women friends decided they had to try it, the trip organizer, Mary Ann, came over to discuss options. Harold and I got out our collection of guidebooks and his topographic maps and started laying out possible itineraries.

"If you spend a day or two at the west end of the Dolomites, you can stay at our favorite hotel, the Armentarola. From there you can start a four-day excursion by hiking to a fabulous private *rifugio*, then two days and nights later you could be at Rifugio Biella—the location is amazing. And the next day you could hike all the way to Cortina."

The Rifugio Biella was founded in 1907, has forty-two beds, and sits at an altitude of 2,327 meters, or 7,634 feet, at the base of the Crodo del Becco, a peak rising further still, to 2,810 meters, or 9,219 feet. Accommodations in the stone structure are basic, with shared rooms and bathrooms—without showers—but the price is right. Harold and I found the food decent enough, and the alpine views could hardly be more breathtaking.

We arranged the various topo maps to illustrate the proposed route. Mary Ann got excited.

"But how do we get back from Cortina to our car at the Armentarola?" she asked, after a moment pondering details.

The air went flat.

"A bus? Or maybe a taxi?" I offered with little enthusiasm.

"Maybe we should just fly over to Italy and pick them up!" said Harold, looking at me.

"That's a great idea!" I agreed.

Mary Ann just looked at us, not sure what to think. But Harold and I had already decided, right on the spot. We were meeting them in the Dolomites at the end of their hike. A minute earlier, we weren't even thinking about going to Italy; now it was a done deal. We loved being impulsive like that.

Even though our trip up Mount Whitney was only a year earlier and involved a climb of more than 6,000 feet and fourteen miles to the 14,000-foot summit, Harold was no longer strong enough for those sorts of treks. But we knew the Dolomites well enough to plan other just as worthwhile hikes he could still handle.

A few days later Sharon called. While we were talking, I mentioned that Harold and I were headed to Italy.

"Really?" she said, drawing out the word, as though she'd just stumbled upon an opportunity. After all, she had. "Would you like some company?"

I was thrilled. She and Graham would join Harold and me in Venice. From there, we'd head to Cortina, where we would pick up our four Healdsburg friends at the end of their walk.

At least that was the initial plan. In Cortina, we had a better idea.

"You know what we should do," I proposed over dinner with Sharon and Graham.

"What's that?" Harold asked, taking a bite of his pasta.

"We should head out a day early and surprise Mary Ann and the gals by hiking to Croda del Becco and the Rifugio Biella!"

Everyone loved the idea. Once again, it was a done deal.

The next day, after hours walking through fields and forests surrounded by the dramatic, exposed rock outcrops typical of the Dolomites, we began the final ascent to Biella. Trees and bushes left behind at the lower elevations, we hiked through green fields littered with gray rocks, the bases of many of the sharp peaks draped in massive slides of them. Occasionally we saw a marmot or cow, a bird of prey circling overhead. The alpine air was fresh and pure.

Suddenly we spied four women leaving a hut and heading up the hill. If it weren't for the green shutters and a glint of sun on the metal roof, I might have missed the stone structure.

In unison, Harold and I ran toward our friends, joyously calling out their names as though reuniting with someone we hadn't seen in years. Like a scene straight out of *The Sound of Music*, as soon as they realized the thin giant in the distance was Harold, all four women came rushing in our direction.

"What a magical mountaintop moment that was," Sharon recalled now, taking another sip of wine.

"One that would have made Julie Andrews proud!" I quipped.

We laughed, but my mind was already moving on to memories that would prove more difficult to relive. Fortunately, Sharon and I had been through enough together. She could let me talk, not trying to distract me or stop my tears—as so often people had been inclined to do.

After spending a wonderful night of conversation and laughter together at the *rifugio*, the next day we all hiked back to the car we had left in Cortina. The sky was blue, the grasses deep green, the temperature mild. Wildflowers lined the trail, and we paused often to take in the breathtaking views. I drank in the crisp mountain air with the same relish I gulped down the cool water from my bottle.

A half hour after getting back to the car, we made the short jaunt to the Hotel Armentarola—the first carload followed by a second—situated in a mountaintop paradise of fragrant conifers and jagged peaks. What began in 1938 as a small guesthouse had long since evolved into a four-star hotel, still run by the same family.

In two waves, we filed inside, our sighs of relief filling the lobby as we set down our gear and sank into comfortable furniture. Polished wood floors below, stained wood ceilings above, antlers lining the walls. Crisp whites and subdued earth tones dominated the sophisticated palette, while rugs and plants added tasteful splashes of color.

After we reluctantly said our goodbyes to the Healdsburg women and Sharon and Graham, Harold and I checked in. We looked forward to a week exploring the region on our own.

In the middle of the night we awoke with a start, the intrusive, merciless ring of a telephone jolting us from our slumber. I propped myself up on one elbow and fumbled around for the receiver.

"Tania?" came a distraught voice.

"Alex?" I said, confused. Why was my brother calling from California?

"She went peacefully."

Mama had died.

My heart broke into pieces. The mother I respected and adored, fought with, and, in the end, took care of, was gone. Her decline had been gradual, starting four years earlier with the onset of dementia. Now it was complete.

How could this be happening, I wondered, overcome with anguish. After all, it wasn't the first time I had missed the death of someone important while in a remote region, disconnected from the outside world.

I needed to go home. I needed to bury Mama, to say goodbye. I needed to be with my brother.

But then I thought of Harold. It was his last visit to these peaks. With every new treatment he lost muscle mass and energy; there was no chance of another trip to his beloved Dolomites. For his sake, I needed to be here.

What I didn't understand was that, like me, he wanted to be with Mama.

As her dementia progressed and she reverted to her native language, Harold could no longer talk with her. No matter. For a time, she thought he was her first lover—and was thrilled to learn I had married him. Regardless of who she thought he was, her face always lit up when he visited. Invariably she wanted to walk with him in the garden or sit and chat—in Serbian.

He, too, loved her very much and needed to say goodbye.

We flew home.

Once there I got my first clue of what it might feel like to lose Harold. I experienced what it meant to lose someone I loved deeply, someone who had been in the process of leaving me for a long time. I learned that, though we might think it easier to let go of someone we know is dying, it's not. There is no dress rehearsal for the final farewell.

The Russian Orthodox religion my mother adopted when she married my father calls for an open casket. In the elaborate, incense-filled cathedral, oblivious to the murmur of the large numbers of people who had come to pay their respects, Harold spent a long time sitting with Mama, holding her hand, talking to her.

Watching them together was almost too much to bear. Seeing Mama like that was hard enough; Harold juxtaposed with her bordered on surreal, an inescapable, gut-wrenching reminder that one would soon follow the other. My heart aching, my limbs weak, I might have looked away if I weren't so concerned for Harold.

What was going through his head? Apart from saying his goodbyes, how could he not be grappling with the ominous awareness that he would be in Mama's place in the not-so-distant future? My body was seized by conflicting impulses. I wanted to rush to Harold's side to comfort him, but I was paralyzed by the thought of inserting myself, of coming face-to-face with what Harold himself had to be facing that very moment. I don't know how or where he found the strength. Then and there, I certainly didn't have it.

Snapping me back to the present, the waiter stopped by with the bill. I dried my eyes with my napkin and reflexively mustered a smile. I had missed my easy tears. It felt good to let them flow with Sharon.

As the waiter walked off with my credit card, I had an insight: I was hungry for experiences, anxious to live life fully before I lost the opportunity, as Mama and Harold had.

Part of me knew I needed to mourn Harold, that it was OK to feel sad, angry, disappointed. Another part knew it was a waste of time to wallow in self-pity when my life was so full of possibility. That part told me to keep moving, to keep living. Both perspectives were legitimate, and this time to reflect with an old friend had helped me see them more clearly. Like our walk down the winding river, my future would unfold one curve at a time. There would be times of mourning. Even more so, there would be times of living.

Sharon and I shared a final drink, then headed to bed. My experience of the Compleat Angler had turned out to be even more special than, only a few hours earlier, I could have possibly imagined.

# Never Say Goodbye

The next day would end near Maidenhead, a town of about 70,000 people. Graham was meeting us for lunch at one of their favorite restaurants.

Thankfully, it would prove to be a short segment of the trail, wooded slopes on the opposite bank ushering us out of Marlow. Sharon and I were both pleasantly drained by all the excitement, food, and drink of the day before. We walked in a mellow glow, chatting about this and that, looking forward to time with Graham.

He and Sharon were heading back to the Cotswolds. I, on the other hand, was only midway through my trip—and it was about to change dramatically.

My plan was to take a train to London, where I would continue my walk past Greenwich all the way to the end of the river, where it meets the ocean. I would base myself in a club in Central London's Sloane Square, from where I would do daily strolls—this time on both sides of the water, as opposed to sticking to whichever side the trail followed. I would walk alone and, rather than quiet country paths surrounded by nature, I'd be in the middle of a thriving city.

Presently, though, it was lunchtime. Sharon and I arrived at the restaurant early, a casual place overlooking the river. Graham joined us shortly after. Time flew as we ate, drank, and talked about our experiences on the trail. Too soon, it was time to head to the train station.

One moment I was hugging Sharon and Graham as

I jumped out of the taxi. The next I was alone for the first time in a week. I wandered through the maze of the station—a hall and crowds and long platforms—and bought a ticket, settling into a seat just as the train began to leave.

Gently rocked by the moving car, wheels on tracks letting out shrill, metal-on-metal screeches as the train struggled to gain momentum, I thought about the notion of parting ways.

Leaving Sharon and Graham had been easy. The train station was crowded, the cab couldn't stop for long, and I would see them again in a few days, when we would end the walk officially at the Thames Barrier.

Linda's departure had been more definitive. I hadn't seen her in years, and we had reconnected in a wonderful way. She was off to distant places, and I didn't know when I would see her again. But as she left us, she had been giddy with excitement, from the walk, fun with the people at the pub, more than a couple of glasses of beer. She had to make a dash for her taxi, limiting our parting to a brief hug, a smile, and a tear on her part. Then off she ran, disheveled and happy.

I didn't say goodbye. Not to Linda. Not to Sharon and Graham. I never do.

My refusal runs deep.

I was raised bilingual. I spoke Russian with my father and Serbian (or Serbo-Croatian as it was called then) with my mother. I learned English as a child, studied German in school, and learned French when I lived in France in my early twenties. In my early fifties I decided to learn Italian.

Of all those languages, only in English do we say "goodbye," which to me has the feel of true parting. In the other languages: *do vidjenja, dosvedanie, arrivederci, au revoir, auf wiedersehn*, the words mean "until we see each other again." Perhaps language itself, then, has also played a part in my not saying goodbye.

If I'm ready to leave a party, I slip out the door, at most giving the host a quick hug, if they aren't too busy with the goings-on.

When Harold was alive, I would say to myself, "He's always with me. I'm not leaving him." I felt and believed it. He was part of me, wherever he was, wherever I was, regardless of whatever the distance ostensibly between us.

It's the same with family and friends. They're a part of me. I leave, they leave, we come back together and share what's important. We don't spend time on the in-between—or the leaving. I don't take people to the airport, to train or bus stations. I never have. Not even Harold—nor did I let him take me. I just left.

Now, though, on the train to London, I needed to reflect on how leaving and living intertwined, on how Harold's leaving me behind impacted who I would become as I went on living.

# No Regrets

In 1987 Harold and I went for a rugged trek through the remote Himalayas of Northern India, from Kashmir to Ladakh, before the area closed to foreigners when fighting between India and Pakistan made it too dangerous.

For the previous four years I had been CEO of a New York Stock Exchange-listed software company in the throes of a messy turnaround. Within days of my stepping into the role—my first position outside of Control Data—the business was hit by multiple shareholder lawsuits and SEC investigations, all the while suffering massive losses. I felt as though I'd been thrown into a cyclone, but I quickly learned I reveled in this kind of high-pressure, high-stakes situation.

My Roundtable support group helped me enormously, as did an amazing lawyer, Bill Dolan, and a staff that, in spite of some very difficult years, kept pushing forward. US laws were changing, and tax benefits relating to losses would evaporate on December 31, 1986. Our own millions in losses were some of our biggest assets—and we risked losing them. Miraculously, mere weeks before the last possible moment, the company was turned around: market share and profitability increased, the lawsuits were settled, and we merged with a firm in Atlanta.

After staying with the post-merger company during the six-month transition period, I needed a break—and I knew exactly what I wanted to do. In the late 1970s I had trekked the Himalayas—in Nepal, around Annapurna, the tenth highest mountain in the world. That first trek was one of the most powerful experiences of my life, and returning would be a way to make a definitive break from the business world. It was August, when there is no trekking in Nepal due to monsoon; but the trekking in Kashmir would be perfect.

I asked Harold to come with me. He really wanted to, but it required a month off from work. His company was trying to float some bonds, and he was deeply involved in that stressful, complicated process. As long as he was working, I reminded him, he would always be involved in something important—there would never be a "good" time to take a break.

"What do you think you'll remember at the end of your life," I asked, "the completion of this bond offering or a trip over the top of the world?"

"Goddamn it," he said. "I hate it when you're right! But sometimes I also love it when you're right. I'm coming."

We started on Dal Lake in Srinagar, where the sunsets were like delicate pastel tapestries. Weaving themselves into ever-evolving displays as the sun sank behind snowcapped mountains, they offered no clue as to what we were about to discover on a boat into nearby waterways.

We found ourselves in a small city, a whole other self-contained world alive with color and humming with sound. Like some sort of Himalayan Venice, here the canals served as roads, wooden boats coming and going in all directions. Some were elaborately carved, topped with canopies draped with fabrics, and painted with bold colors; others were weathered, their paint faded and peeling. All were piloted from the back, often by men in long cloaks. From our own boat, we observed restaurants and retailers and convenience stores where bags of chips hung like garlands, right on the waterfronts, awaiting patrons who boated all the way up to their doorsteps.

The women we saw wore outlandish quilts of patterns, multilayered outfits haphazardly thrown together, each design clashing with the others. There were no solids, just a riot of motifs wrapped in complex origami folds that would have made Moschino proud. Children were everywhere, and they were just as striking, the chaotic spectacle infused with their bright smiles and boundless energy.

We stayed on beautiful houseboats. Like so many of the smaller boats we'd seen, these, too, had elaborate woodwork, reminding me of the craftmanship I'd seen on old Russian dachas, intricate, gingerbread-house detailing. Had we thought these pleasing abodes with their familiar, welcome amenities were a precursor of things to come, we would have been wrong. It was the last we saw of luxury and comfort for a long time.

Walking for days through mountains of green terraces, going higher and higher, we passed through small villages and peeked into sacred shrines, modest places of worship that added unexpected bursts of color to our path. Their walls often painted in eye-catching reds and golds, the shrines sometimes featured depictions of the elephant-god Ganesh or multi-armed Shiva or any number of other fantastical Hindu deities.

Eventually the land became barren, and we found ourselves among Muslims, with whom we would spend the next week. The people here were quieter than many of those we had encountered thus far, though still warm and friendly. Their clothes, too, were more sober than their predecessors'. Traditionally dressed men and women wore shirts—usually a solid color, green, black, or blue—that hung to the knees and covered loose-fitting pants. They also donned curious head coverings that almost resembled towels, leaving visible their faces and much of their hair. Other men and boys wore long-sleeve button-downs or sweaters and pants that, almost without exception, were dirty. Few people wore shoes.

Not only were the villagers welcoming, but they graciously invited us into their mosques. I was surprised when the invitation extended to me as well, even though I was a woman.

One mosque in particular made a lasting impression. Despite the poverty of its community, which was encircled by barren, rocky mountainsides; despite the drab, dusty streets outside, somehow the mosque was an immaculate, lively green, decorated with white and red wood trim. The structure had two brick minarets that took to the sky, each the tawny color of the surroundings—except for the green, red, and gold of striking mosaics near the top, the towers' uppermost reaches capped with onion domes surprisingly reminiscent of those found on Russian Orthodox churches. Loudspeakers clung to one of the towers, ensuring no one in the village forgot their five-times-daily prayers.

Inside the mosque was no less appealing. While eager young men accompanied us—eventually posing for a group photo—we observed elegant floral motifs painted against a backdrop of bold yellow. The same color was used for what I assumed were Koranic verses over the otherwise green mihrab, the niche indicating the direction of Mecca, toward which Muslims are instructed to pray.

When, having left behind our new Muslim friends, we reached the highest passes, the mountains were brown as far as the eye could see—except where snow glowed white. Here Buddhists walked barren fields with their yaks. The Buddhists spun the thick yak wool into dark burgundy robes worn by both men and women. In their tiny settlements, never far from streams of glacial runoff, they grew short-season crops. In spite of the harsh conditions, they seemed surprisingly well fed and, at least to us outsiders, content.

Our group was much less so. Yes, Harold and I were enjoying the unforgettable sights. But our trip organizers were woefully unprepared for our rugged adventure—and did little to ensure that our fellow travelers were either.

Some Australians had shown up wearing tennis shoes and dungarees, when what they really needed were heavy hiking boots and warm, waterproof clothing. The organizers didn't prevent the Australians from joining, and they suffered terribly. Several left in the middle of the trek, when we were a two-day walk from a Tibetan truck route.

An even more problematic issue was the organizers' failure to pack enough food. The remoteness meant locals couldn't sell us much to make up for what we lacked. Things got even worse when a donkey carrying eight boxes of sixty-four eggs each slipped on one of the narrow mountain trails. All 500 eggs perished.

Harold and the other men lost so much weight that soon they had to tie their belts instead of buckle them. Harold was thin to begin with: at 6'6" he only weighed about 180 pounds. It was concerning to watch him lose nearly thirty pounds.

For some reason, initially we women didn't lose much weight. That eventually changed for me. After eating potatoes for three meals a day for much of the trip, I got to the point where I could no longer stand the sight of them. The pounds began to melt away.

The equipment was terrible. The tents leaked. We ate off tarps on the ground, sitting on folding camp stools with no backs. Every few meals we'd be interrupted by an agonized cry as yet another stool buckled under one of the guy's weight, the metal bar between the stool legs jabbing a particularly painful spot between the man's.

The night before our big climb over a nearly 18,000-foot pass, it stormed, making for slow going the next day. The rainfall turned the final river into a raging, swollen snow melt that took extra time to cross. It was dark before we set up camp. When the pack animals ran off into the night, we were left without food after the long and difficult day.

And yet.

It was the trip of a lifetime.

Every challenge made us stronger.

And Harold and I did it together.

When we reached the end of the trek at Leh, Ladakh, for centuries an important stopover on trade routes between Tibet, Kashmir, India, and China, our dingy hotel felt like Shangri La. Like most buildings in the dusty town, just a few stories tall, through our window we saw dramatic barren peaks—not a single patch of green in sight. When we happened upon a restaurant that served—of all things—banana pancakes, we ended up going five, six, even seven times a day.

We needed the calories not only to put some weight back onto Harold's frightfully skinny bones, but to do some quick sightseeing. Ladakh is a land of temples, and we were pleased to discover Leh boasted ones not to be missed.

Located on a hilltop with breathtaking views of the Himalaya, the Paldan Lumo Temple impressed us with its intricate wall paintings and pillars covered with tiger hides. At Red Maitreya we marveled at a sixty-five-foot-tall Buddha statue, as well as the temple's joyful colors and elaborate wood carvings.

We reveled in our good fortune and fascinating wanderings until we learned that the person who should have had our plane tickets had gotten drunk and absconded with the money. We had no reservations. We could have worked around that, since on these trips Harold and I always carried large sums of cash in case we had to be helicoptered out. The problem was that bad weather meant there were no flights for days.

We tried to hire jeeps, but they wouldn't take dollars. We went to banks. They wouldn't change our money.

"The road is closed, and the phones are down," the teller explained, a thin, older man in a white button-down. He had gray hair and thick glasses. "We do not have any way of finding out the exchange rate."

The lobby was small and simple. A counter. Dusty tile floors that were chipped in places. A few yellowing posters that appeared to have been on the walls for decades.

"Can't you use yesterday's rate?" I proposed.

"No, we are not allowed to do this."

"We'd be happy to pay a premium over yesterday's rate, to make sure you don't have a problem." Harold offered.

"We are very sorry, sir," repeated the bank manager, who materialized out of nowhere, not quite as old and considerably heavier than the teller. Polite but unwavering, he repeated, "We cannot change your money until the road opens or the line is fixed."

After more asking around, we finally found a couple of jeep drivers who would take our dollars. Fit and friendly, dressed in active wear better suited to the demands of their job than traditional village garb, the two young Buddhists were also confident in their abilities—crucial, since the road on which we were about to embark was one of the most dangerous in the world, winding through some of the most extreme mountain terrain on Earth. Getting from one end to the other would require not only skill honed through experience but nerves of steel.

The next morning we set off on our two-day drive.

Comprised of little more than dirt and rocks, the landscape supported almost no vegetation. Even the snow that had once covered it—still occasionally visible on the distant, higher elevations—no longer found it hospitable.

The road was unpaved, bumpy, and so narrow in places that I couldn't help but repeatedly close my eyes in terror. My fear was justified. When I did muster the courage to look down the treacherous mountainsides, I saw countless cars and trucks abandoned to their fate—one I hoped would not be our own. Boulders that had fallen onto the road offered little reassurance, creating obstacles to circumvent and acting as troublesome reminders of the very real dangers along the route.

Our drivers were about to offer even more insight into those dangers.

"This time last year a major storm hit a caravan of

many vehicles," one of the young men began, as though making casual conversation. "The cars were all trapped in the snow."

"But, it's August," I protested, wondering if he had got his dates wrong.

"Yes, August," he insisted. "So a bigger surprise to have snow."

"How many cars?" Harold wondered.

"There were several hundred, sir. They were all going in a convoy to Srinagar, as we are."

"Several *hundred*!" I blurted out.

I looked at Harold, as though asking what to do, as though maybe we should stop and get out or perhaps even turn around. Waiting a few days for a plane no longer seemed like such an inconvenience.

"What happened to them?" Harold asked, taking my hand.

"They were buried by the snow, sir. It snowed for days and days. Then it was too cold and deep to get them out."

"So, how long before they *did* get out?"

"They did not get out, sir. Nobody got out."

Our driver's English was sketchy. We tried to convince ourselves that the language barrier had resulted in some sort of misunderstanding. After all, if there actually had been a disaster of that magnitude, surely we would have heard about it, even as far away as the States, right?

A silence descended on the jeep.

I didn't let go of Harold's hand.

It wasn't until much later, safe at home after our trip, that we would confirm we hadn't misunderstood our drivers. Neither had they been exaggerating. Several hundred people had perished in an unseasonable barrage of snowfall that buried them alive.

One potential danger with which, thankfully, we did not have to contend was oncoming traffic. No surprise perhaps that vehicles could only travel in one direction at a time. After four hours, we had to call it a day, so that traffic could flow in the direction from which we had just arrived.

Other than the countless vehicles, our stopping point consisted of just a handful of houses. Our drivers knew a family who kindly provided us a luxury afforded only a very few lucky travelers: they let us spend the night on their floor. At that point anything was better than more death-defying teetering on the edge of a cliff at the top of the world. I relished the solid surface and slept like a baby in my sleeping bag, exhausted from our long, harrowing journey.

The next day we made it to Srinagar, before continuing to Delhi.

Until his final months, Harold and I would talk about that trip, one of the high points of our lives. Laughing, he would always say, "You know, I have no idea what I was working on at the time. But I remember every breath, every day, every challenge we encountered—and there were so many! I have never once regretted that decision."

# Always Here

The night before our plane out of Delhi, I decided to call Mama. Harold and I lived in Minnesota at the time, but we were stopping over in San Francisco to see her and my father.

She answered in a voice I barely recognized.

"*Njega vise nema*," she kept repeating, her words that much harder to comprehend, given the wire static and delay.

In a long room lit only by the flicker of yak-butter candles, Harold and I had sat listening to the hypnotic chants of fifty Buddhist monks, each dressed in simple wool robes of maroon and saffron. Meanwhile, unbeknownst to us, 10,000 miles away the smell of incense filled the nave of a large, candlelit cathedral. Mourners listened to the solemn bass intonations of the Russian Orthodox priest—long, white beard, ornate robe brocaded in gilt—as he, too, chanted, albeit for an altogether different occasion.

My father's funeral liturgy.

"He is no longer here," my mother said again.

He had died while we were on our remote trip.

Weeks ago.

How was it possible that I'd had no premonition, no hint of loss, not the faintest disturbance to the deep peace that overcomes me in the sanctity of those mountains?

It didn't matter. Only one thing did: a lifetime of our issues unresolved, he was gone.

The outfitter, along with their other transgressions, hadn't made any effort to let us know—even though they did. The president of my company had contacted them many times in an urgent attempt to find us. Even once we made it to Ladakh, where communications were much easier, the outfitter couldn't be bothered to share with us the devastating news.

I hung up the telephone, clung to Harold, and sobbed, reduced to my five-year-old self, unable to fathom how my smiling, playful Papa could possibly not only be dead but already buried—while I had missed it all.

When I left on the trip, he was an active seventy-year-old whose latest physical had confirmed a clean bill of health. Early one morning a week later, he got up to go fishing on the San Francisco Bay and collapsed of a heart attack by the side of the bed. A few hours later he was dead.

And I wasn't there to say goodbye.

Not just to say goodbye, but for any of it. Not to support and comfort my Mama or brother. Not to receive their support and comfort. Not for the reality to sink in, so my mourning could begin.

In a state of shock, my feelings ran amok, a confusing mix of sadness, anger, and guilt. I suddenly loathed New Delhi and had to get home. I had to be with my mother.

It wasn't until my return to San Francisco that I learned firsthand what it meant to have missed my father's funeral. I had lost that exquisite moment when I could feel sorry for myself or berate myself for not being the perfect daughter that, in an ideal world, I would have been for him. I missed the opportunity to apologize and thank him and cry with those who also loved him. I forfeited that briefest of moments when his death was the only thing that mattered, that moment before life moved into a future that forever relegated my father to the past.

---

We had a stormy relationship, my father and I.

As a child I adored him. As a teenager I resented this stern, strict man whose English was never very good, who was unable not only to settle into life as an American, but to make the transition to being an American father.

Why couldn't I go to a bowling alley? Really? I was a teenager, and it was the place to be—all my friends spent time there. But in my house it was held in suspicious contempt, each visit sure to obliterate more of my morals, like a ball striking pin after pin until not one is left standing. The only way I could go was when I sometimes managed to sneak away without my parents knowing.

And why couldn't I go to a dance when all my friends did? Saint Tania Day was one of the biggest holidays on the Russian calendar. Every year there was a ball where the entire community celebrated all the Tanias. I desperately wanted to go—to have my moment in the spotlight, be one of the stars—but my father declared it out of the question until I was eighteen. By the time that came around, I had abandoned the Russian community and no longer had any interest in being a belle of the ball.

Then of course there was the incident in the backseat of the car.

Sometimes it feels as though I spent my entire childhood fighting. I was determined to speak my mind, and doing so invariably entailed endless arguments and shouting matches. It seemed I had to fight my way through life, that otherwise no one would let me succeed. I had to fight to be me: with the men in my family, especially on the Russian side; with a mother who criticized my appearance, urged me to hide behind the scenes, and insisted that if I were more like my "adopted brother" Alec, I would be more loveable; with the kids at grammar school who resented my being the smart one—so much so, that one day I ended up face down on the playground.

As middle-class white families moved out of San Francisco in the 1950s, more and more empty homes were left behind, lowering their values. Over time, those neighborhoods started filling with Black families. Once that happened, white flight accelerated. But Blacks weren't the only ones to benefit from the new opportunities: the departure of the middle class also created housing openings for poor immigrant families like mine.

The changes in the student-body make-up at my elementary school, Andrew Jackson, reflected our neighborhood's evolution. When the school opened in 1913 it was almost exclusively white. As late as 1950, very few Black families lived in the neighborhood, but by 1964 the percentage of Black students was sixty-six percent. It rose to seventy-three percent in 1969.

In my parents' eyes my new school represented a step forward, yet another opportunity afforded us by our adopted country and city. In reality, the superficial image of a schoolyard full of children laughing, playing hopscotch, kickball, and basketball, and otherwise making the most of their innocent, exuberant youth was a far cry from my more complicated daily reality.

Almost immediately I began to perceive the deep biases that surrounded me, at home and school alike. My teachers—all of whom were white—were mostly supportive. But there were few white kids in my class, and my father was not keen on my becoming friends with the Black ones, especially the boys.

I tried to make friends with the few white girls. When I grew close to a girl named Betty, her mother decided she shouldn't hang around me, a foreigner—and a Russian one at that. She didn't want her daughter becoming friends with "one of those Communists." Betty's cousin, Lois, was in our class, and they started spending all their time together—leaving me out.

It didn't matter that I was a refugee from Communism, not a Communist myself. Betty was taught that all Russians were Communists—and therefore bad. I had to be avoided at all costs. It broke my heart. From then on, my friends were mostly limited to my Russian crowd outside of school.

As hurtful as that was, my pain wasn't just emotional; it also became physical.

Every time I set foot in the schoolyard I put myself at risk. It took years to get over the fear of it, a fear that was not imagined. To the contrary, when a well-aimed basketball smacked against the back of my head, I went down, knocked unconscious. Not surprisingly, I don't remember what happened after that. In fact, the trauma was such that I even forgot about the incident itself until weeks later, when severe headaches forced me to miss school. It was only when I was taken to a radical new kind of healthcare professional—a chiropractor—that we discovered a bone in the back of my neck had been thrust out of place, bringing back a memory both physically and emotionally painful.

If I were going to survive in such an environment, I had to toughen up. And so I did. When the schoolyard bullies tried to push me around, I pushed back, catching them off guard and earning their respect. Once they realized I wasn't going anywhere, that I wasn't going to hide or let them mess with me, they accepted me as an equal, a petite, blonde "tough guy" rather than a defenseless, cowering underdog.

The tall Black boys at Andrew Jackson forced this little white immigrant girl to learn to stand up for herself. It was a survival skill that would come in handy when, as I began my professional career, I again found myself the odd one out, a young woman fighting to make her way in a man's world.

After my teen years, my father and I were never again close—at least not while he was alive.

What I had no way of knowing was that my relationship with Papa would continue to evolve. As strange as it might sound, we grew closer after his death. Writing my book *One Hundred Years of Exile: A Romanov's Search for Her Father's Russia* was a healing endeavor that brought us even closer, giving me deeper insight into his experience and how it informed our relationship while he was alive.

Years after his passing, once again I found myself on a long trek in the Himalayas. High in those beloved mountains where I had been when he died, I had a vivid, joyous dream. He was there with me in the highlands, alive and happy. I knew with certainty that he loved me, that he forgave me for all the turbulent times in our relationship.

Coming to understand that even after death people don't disappear without a trace, but instead continue to be active and present in a different way, has been one of life's greatest spiritual lessons. It has been a comfort as I've lost others close to me.

It would be yet again, when I lost Harold.

# Better than Goodbye

Harold and I fought his prostate cancer for sixteen years.

Sixteen miraculous years that made a mockery of the original prognosis of just one and a half, based on the aggressive return of the cancer after surgery that failed to do away with it.

Harold tried many different treatments. They would work to varying degrees, but the cancer would always come back. Another strategy always had to be found. Meanwhile, he endured ongoing hormone therapy, sapping him of his strength. Additional treatments placed still more of a burden on his body.

In spite of it all, somehow Harold continued to live a very active life. He became a long-distance bicycle rider. He spent winter months skiing; in the summer he swam laps in the pool. He did strength training and took up Pilates. He hiked. It was as if by keeping his bones so strong he denied the cancer a foothold to eat away at them.

And yet the cancer continued its slow, relentless progression, the chemo leaving Harold ever more exhausted and thin to gauntness.

On our return from a 2011 trip to Hawaii, familiar problems reoccurred: heart arrhythmia and severe shortness of breath. We spent several frustrating days in the emergency room. I kept thinking how, for the first time in my life, I had more money than time.

After the interminable limbo at the hospital, I threw

the money around in desperation, madly reorganizing our world. I set up an outdoor living room on our bedroom deck, so Harold had less need to go downstairs. I had a handrail installed in the pool. I bought expensive, comfortable lounge furniture. I found the highest quality king-size bed, one on which the mattress firmness could be adjusted to protect Harold's "bony ass," as I now lovingly referred to it. To further protect those bones, a soft seat was added to the toilet. The rest of the bathroom was refitted with handrails.

My efforts helped ease Harold's discomfort. They did not interrupt the disease's progression. A scan showed the cancer continued to spread through his bones, lymph nodes, and, even, his brain—though not yet extensively. All the same, we decided he could not undergo another series of chemo. At 150 pounds, his body simply could not take any more. The doctors gave him six months to live.

Beth and the kids were scheduled to visit three days later. I told them Harold was really struggling—they should come now. When Brad called, we decided he and his family should also join us right away.

The house filled with little grandchildren. They snuggled their beloved Papa, who was soon unable leave the bed. The hospice nurse began preparing us for the end, explaining Harold had maybe a few weeks left.

"I can't believe he's going to die," Beth lamented, one night when she and I were standing alone in the kitchen. The dishwasher hummed behind her.

"I know," I agreed, tears welling in my eyes.

"No, really," she insisted. "I can't believe it. How did it come to this?"

"What do you mean, Beth? We've always known that

it would." I pulled a chair out from under the kitchen table. I let myself slump into it.

"Have we?" Beth countered, digging in her heels. "You guys have barely even talked about it for so long—it's been like he wasn't even sick anymore."

I saw then that our odds-defying history with the disease had, in a sense, been misleading—and left the family unprepared. We had turned a year and a half into sixteen and had every intention of continuing to outdo ourselves. It was understandable that Beth and other family and friends might have lost sight of the still-every-bit-as-true reality of the situation. She was right, after all: Harold and I hadn't made a point of reminding everyone he was still dying. Did we really need to? What was the point? It had never occurred to us that, by not discussing it regularly, people might start believing what they wanted to believe.

When, in the blink of an eye, six months turned into mere days, we found out just how ill-prepared we were for such a brutal reversal of fortune.

Beth and Brad prolonged their stays. The spouses and grandkids went home. I asked Harold's closest friends to come see him one last time. I remembered how important it had been for him to say goodbye a couple of years earlier to his friend Jack, even if the best we could do then was a phone call from Morocco.

That night we shared our new bed: Harold, his catheter, his meds, and me. He couldn't turn his body, but I could still cuddle up to his warmth, his love. I wrapped my arms over his chest, raised one leg gently over his, and cupped his bony ass in as close to a full-body embrace as I could manage.

The next morning I woke up still glued to him, as

though having no intention of ever letting him go. The room glowed with morning sun. Birds outside the window celebrated the dawn of a new day. Harold breathed calmly and quietly, my arm rising and falling on his back like a piece of driftwood on the sea.

With a gentle smile, eventually he woke. He wasn't in pain and could breathe, so we reduced his meds and shared a quiet morning together. He read the paper, I read a book. We chatted, we did nothing. We savored the precious time together, taking not a single moment for granted.

Our friend Yvonne came to visit, as did my sister-in-law Renée. My brother Alex, Harold's closest friend, had left a few days earlier for Kauai, where he was rebuilding a house. At the time Harold had seemed stable.

Beth, Brad, and I had not been out of the house in days. Since Harold was having a good morning—in relative terms, at least—we decided to take a walk down the driveway.

We went into the bedroom to tell him we were leaving. Beth leaned over and kissed him.

He smiled his familiar smile. Then he looked at all of us and quietly said, "I love you."

"We'll see you soon," I said, giving him another kiss and a light squeeze of the hand as we left the room.

---

We lived deep in the woods, our driveway extending a quarter mile. The section that approached the road at the bottom of the hill was in a cellular dead zone. Shortly after we turned to make the climb back up to the house, my phone pinged. I had a voicemail.

"Harold is going. Please, please, come back," Renée urged.

In a panic, I raced to my neighbors' porch, desperate to get a ride back up the hill. Just then other neighbors drove up. Brad, Beth, and I piled into their car, frantically explaining what was going on.

When we got to the house, we jumped out of the car and raced to the door, to the bedroom, to the bed, to Harold.

Who was gone.

Our last kiss. Our last touch.

His last "I love you."

Little could we have known.

He had waited until we left for our walk, then slipped away peacefully. Like when I don't want to disturb the host, he had left the party early, without saying goodbye.

But then, "I love you" is so much better than goodbye.

I understood his choice was intentional. He wanted me to feel that he really was gone. He wanted me to come home to that realization, that reality, that experience of an unmistakable before and after.

---

My father. My mother. Harold.

As I look back, I wonder if the disappearance in my absence of the three people closest to me was something I somehow willed to happen. As though watching them go were more than I could bear, would trigger agonizing feelings of abandonment. Surely it must have contributed to why I felt so numb and empty dealing with their deaths.

I thought about all this as I sat in the train heading

for London, a dynamic city that would be full of people, but where I would continue the Thames Path unaccompanied.

It occurred to me that time alone was just as important as time with loved ones, but that it would be unbearable if I had no friends or family awaiting my return. I worried that, now that I was single, I might be alone too much or travel so often that friends would forget about me.

Mostly, though, I hoped I could take this time for myself to figure out who I was, now that I was truly on my own.

# Part Two:
# Walking Alone

# Oversharing

I knew London well. But I wasn't here to revisit familiar, beloved sites; I was here to finish my walk along the Thames Path National Trail.

As I was about to find out, much as the trek itself was an exploration of difficult, unknown parts of myself, so, too, would the trail reveal to me a novel perspective on previously unknown parts of the city.

The logistics here were simpler than in the countryside. Since it made no sense to change accommodations each night, I would do the walk in segments, returning to my starting point at the end of each outing. The next morning I would take public transportation to wherever I'd left off the day before and continue from there.

I began my first day by strolling through Sloane Square, past Venus holding her perpetually flowing shell on one end and, on the other, the tall war memorial cross. As it had for most of my walk with Sharon and Linda, the weather cooperated, characterized by slightly overcast skies and unseasonably warm temperatures.

Proceeding onto tree-lined Chelsea Bridge Road, I reveled in its gorgeous brick townhomes, each with elegant entryways and iron railings. One and then another double-decker bus passed as I followed the busy street, which took me all the way to its namesake bridge, the first self-anchored suspension bridge in Britain. As I would later learn, it was built entirely with materials sourced from within the British Empire.

Cars, buses, and motorbikes rushed by. Pigeons scuttled about at my feet, seagulls squawked overhead. The longer I walked, the harder it became to shake the feeling that something was off. Maybe more than one thing, in fact.

Instead of birdsong, I heard motors and horns and, even, a jackhammer. On the sometimes-crowded sidewalks, people called out. They hollered into cell phones. After our idyllic, carefree walks in the countryside, the shift to this hyper-urban, frenzied cityscape threw me off balance. Seized by a sort of culture shock, my system was going to need a day or two to acclimate.

Leaving behind the bridge, on the opposite shore I saw a massive red-brick structure. Four square towers rose to the sky, supporting four white smokestacks that reached higher still. The scene was oddly reminiscent of the large mosques that dominate Istanbul's skyline. And while this building had indeed become its own sort of place of worship—a shopping mall—it owed its monumental size and distinctive form to its original incarnation: the Battersea Power Station.

Closer to the truth would be to call it the Battersea Power Stations, since the complex is actually the site of not one but two nearly identical plants, which accounts for its symmetry and four smokestacks. Both stations were decommissioned in the 1970s, after which it would be decades before the iconic buildings were repurposed to house office and retail space, as well as residences.

I spent a while passing through an area of townhomes and apartment buildings. Across the water, modern high-rises popped up. The road eventually veered away from the river, and it wasn't until I came to a busy intersection and glanced to my right that I realized I had come to Vauxhall Bridge. Careful to navigate the bikers, buses, and automobile traffic coming at me on all sides, I found my way through the cacophony and billows of exhaust, heading for a closer look at the bridge.

Consisting of five steel arches, the bridge's red and yellow paint caught my eye. I also admired one of the two bronze statues on the bridge's center piers, a woman dressed in classical garb and carrying a large pot. She was known as *Agriculture, Architecture, Engineering and Pottery*. Her sister, *Science, Fine Arts, Local Government and Education*, carried a bundle of grain and graced the downstream piers.

Even more eye-catching than the bridge was what I spied on the other side of it: the home of British intelligence, MI6. I recognized it immediately from the movies.

Though impressive in size, to me the building always seemed to try too hard. A cumbersome, contemporary structure, I couldn't help but think it would be more at home in the burbs. Its boxy hodgepodge of tiers and turrets reminded me of a giant cake made of Legos. Its blue glass wings looked like unimaginative add-ons no one was supposed to notice. I tried not to.

Shortly after came The Tate Britain, the oldest gallery in the network of Tate museums, which includes the renowned Tate Modern. This Tate, however, had nothing modern about it. Its classical portico dramatically recalled ancient Rome or Greece, complete with monumental columns and a pediment regally crowned with a trio of statues symbolizing the United Kingdom: a lion, a unicorn, and the figure of Britannia. No surprise that the museum itself—as the name also suggests—focuses on British art.

It turns out the museum has almost as storied a history as its collection. Being right on the Thames meant that some of the pieces were damaged when the river overspilled its banks. The building itself suffered bomb damage during World War II. Thankfully, most of the collection was safe, in storage elsewhere during the war—with one notable exception. When a particular painting was deemed too large to move, someone had the ingenious idea of protecting it with a custom-built brick wall.

When I learned that the museum restaurant had been closed due to protests over a mural's depiction of the enslavement of Black children and for stereotyping the Chinese, I was reminded of similar recent controversies at home.

Still more skyscrapers appeared on the opposite riverbank, and soon I passed Millbank Pier, where I could have caught a boat to the Tate Modern. That would come later. For now, I had my eye set on a bench under a tree in front of Millbank Tower. A glass and steel structure, its architecture, indistinct other than the fact that it ascended to much greater heights than its neighbors, offered little clue as to the high-profile tenants who came and went through its doors, from the Labour and Conservative parties to the United Nations and World Bank.

I took a seat on the bench and beheld the view opening up before me, including Lambeth Bridge. As I did, it occurred to me that the river, which had been so central to my trek thus far, now somehow felt less consequential.

True, I was strolling along its banks—it was right there, just as it had been when Sharon, Linda, and I were going from village to village. Yet, whereas before it had been the winding thread that held everything together, now it almost seemed upstaged, lost in the commotion as my senses were assaulted by the constant barrage of sights and smells, of things piquing my curiosity and grabbing my attention. The trail now felt less like a river walk and more like an urban hike. I was in a city I loved, but I couldn't deny feeling a little disappointed, as though part of me had been left behind in the countryside.

My nostrils inhaling something fishy, my eyes shifted to the bridge. Like its predecessor, the structure consisted of five arches. Other than red trim, however, this bridge was less interesting visually. Pairs of obelisks embellished both ends, topped by stone pinecones adding a little more flair—and spawning an urban myth. The pinecones were rumored actually to be pineapples, in tribute to John Tradescant the Younger, said to have grown the first pineapple in Britain.

An older gentleman took a seat next to me, shifting my attention yet again, this time to my personal space. In his mid- to late-seventies, he had silver hair, rosy cheeks, and a full belly. He wore a tan cardigan and shuffled about in well-worn loafers. He had to be somebody's grandfather. I moved over a little to make room.

Before I knew it, I was telling him about my trek, about my loss, about Harold. I don't know what came over me. Perhaps, without Linda and Sharon around, I was feeling lonelier than I realized. Perhaps it was specifically because he was a stranger—someone who would listen with no context or judgement or any possibility of ever again bringing up any of what I shared. I'm not sure. All I know is that, unable to help myself, it wasn't long before tears were welling up in my eyes.

"We could share a coffee, if that would make you feel better," the man said, putting his arm around me, his breath too close for comfort. "I'm happy to give you a shoulder to cry on."

Alarm bells went off. What was I doing? How foolish could I be?

"Thanks, but I'm meeting a friend—and I'm running late," I lied, before rushing off.

As I put distance between the stranger and myself, it occurred to me that, in a sense, I had come a long way—from sharing almost nothing to sharing just about everything with almost anyone!

Inevitably, I also found myself thinking about Hawaii.

# A Loose Woman

It was the last summer before I finished college at Berkeley. I decided I wanted to spend it someplace special. After some thought, I called the university's employment placement office and told them I was interested in an opportunity in Alaska.

A few weeks later, the phone rang.

"We have the perfect summer job for you!" a woman from the employment office explained. From the tone of her voice, I imagined her on the edge of her seat.

"Oh my god," I exclaimed, her excitement infectious. "You found me something in Alaska!"

"No, not Alaska—someplace even better!" she replied, scarcely able to contain herself, "Hawaii!"

The job was as a summer tour guide at Waimea Falls, on O'ahu's North Shore. The pay was meager initially, but— the woman explained, now practically out of breath—performance-based increases would kick in quickly. And although the employer was not paying travel expenses, they would provide housing.

It wasn't Alaska, but it was too good to turn down.

Several weeks later I was living with seven other Berkeley coeds in a North Shore beach house and leading hikes along trails beneath the falls. Warm sunshine, clear skies, salty breezes. As I looked across the deep-blue ocean at the limitless horizon, I couldn't help feeling it was going to be a summer to remember.

The job required that my housemates and I take turns making the two-and-a-half-hour trip to the main office in Honolulu, where we had administrative duties. A couple of weeks into the engagement, I was the first chosen for the task.

When I arrived in Honolulu, I was greeted with a daunting amount of work. As the day wore on and evening approached, it was clear I wasn't going to get to it all.

"That's fine," my boss, Bob, offered. In his late twenties or early thirties, he was tall, a little overweight, and had short sandy hair and a round, pockmarked face. "If you want, we could take a break for dinner, and you could come back after. There's a bed in the back room, so you can sleep here tonight and head back to the Falls in the morning."

After a quick dinner nearby at an inexpensive restaurant, we returned to the office. As Bob went to leave, he also went in for the kill. Before I knew what hit me, I found myself wrapped in an unwelcome, sensual embrace, one clearly intended as a prelude to intimacy in which I had no interest.

A defensive rush of adrenaline kicking in, I pushed him off me, took a step back, and—as calmly as I could, given the circumstances—said goodnight. My heart was racing, my senses on high alert. While Bob looked away, deciding his next move, I looked at my surroundings, assessing the best way to defend myself, were it to come to that.

Message received, Bob turned to go. No sooner had he closed the door than I made sure it was locked behind him. As my limbs continued to tremble and my mind to race, I listened to each step he took down the hall, holding my breath until I was convinced he had gotten onto the elevator. I then collapsed into a chair, trying to process what had just happened and wondering what to do next.

I was in a city where I didn't know anyone, and I didn't have enough money for a hotel. Bob had listened when I said no and left without putting up a fight. The door was locked, and the room with the bed also had a lock, albeit a simple one.

The more I thought about it, the more I felt OK sleeping in the office. The sad truth, after all, was that I didn't see any other option. I would just make sure to be gone long before Bob returned in the morning.

Little could I know that Bob would be back long before that.

---

I awoke to the sound of the doorknob rattling. The room was dark, so I couldn't see it. But I could hear it.

"Tania. It's Bob. Can you open the door?"

I jumped out of bed as though he were already in the room. For all I knew, he was about to be.

"No," I called back, my voice as unsteady as my limbs. My head spinning, in a surreal limbo between half-asleep and full-on panic, I added, "What are you doing, Bob? I'm sleeping."

"Tania," he insisted, his voice more stern this time, "open the door."

What I did instead was grab a chair and prop it under the doorknob.

"Bob, it's late," I implored. "Please just go away."

"Tania, let me in!" he demanded, jiggling the doorknob yet again.

"No! I am *not* letting you in!" I shouted. "Leave me alone!"

There was no phone in the room. Cell phones didn't even exist yet. If Bob managed to get through the door, my only option would be to fight. He was a tall, heavyset man. I was a short, petite woman. The odds were not in my favor.

A loud smack against the door made me jump, sending another wave of alarm through my body. I prayed the door would hold, that he wasn't about to kick it in.

A prolonged and indecipherable silence followed. Then he left. I might not have known, if he hadn't slammed the door behind him.

After waiting a few more moments to make sure he truly was gone, I crumbled onto the bed. Was I safe? Had he really given up, or would he be back for a third attempt? Should I leave? If I tried, would he be waiting for me? In the lobby downstairs? Outside around a corner, lunging at me from the shadows?

It didn't matter, I reminded myself yet again. I didn't have anywhere else to go.

I didn't sleep a wink the rest of the night.

---

The sun's rays were barely perceptible when I left the office. The dark streets were empty, other than a couple of stray cats and some garbage collectors, the air reeking of truck exhaust and putrefying waste. I headed for the station and caught the first bus back to the North Shore.

My return to the house, however, did not mean a return to safety.

"Tania!" Bob called from downstairs. "Where is Tania?"

Once again I was jolted awake, paralyzed with fear. It was mid-morning, the sun sneaking in around the edges of the window blinds. One of the gals was having breakfast. She told Bob I was upstairs.

"Tania, get down here now!"

The last thing I wanted was to see him again. I hadn't even begun to process—let alone recover from—the night before. But he was the boss. And I was in his house.

My chest tight, my throat dry, with belabored steps I plodded downstairs. Face to face with an enraged Bob, my heart beat so loudly I hardly heard anything he said. But I got the message. I no longer had a job. I no longer had a place to stay.

"And don't come back!" he warned, before storming out of the house.

"What happened?" asked one of the girls.

"Are you OK?" asked another, who had appeared on the stairs when she heard the commotion.

I was confused. I was ashamed. The girls were nice, but I barely knew them. We had been together a mere two weeks. And, given everything that had just happened, I was reluctant to trust anyone.

Anyone except the Millers.

Dr. Miller and his wife lived next door with two young daughters. While it was true that I didn't know them well either, the entire family had been friendly since my arrival—and I really needed the company and support of some adults.

No place else to turn, I walked over to their house.

Mrs. Miller gave me a shoulder to cry on, as well as a safe place to get some rest. She also sent one of her daughters over to the house for my things. When Dr. Miller came home that evening, he took their kindness to a whole other level.

"Both the girls could really use a math tutor. How would you feel about living with us this summer in exchange for tutoring them?"

He didn't have to ask twice.

My time at the Miller's was delightful. I tutored the girls, both of whom were not only sweet but also quick studies. To earn extra cash, I put my sewing skills to use, making and selling bikinis.

Things got even better when my boyfriend, Greg, showed up on our doorstep without notice. Greg had been in the middle of playing tournaments on the European tennis circuit. He gave it up to come to my aid.

Yet again Dr. Miller rose to the occasion, quickly finding a dilapidated old beach bungalow where Greg and I could spend the summer.

Each night when we returned home, the road to the house was covered with so many bufo toads that they squished under our tires for the entire ride.

"It's so gross!" Greg and I would laugh.

Inside the house almost as many geckos covered the window screens, which I also found unsettling. Nothing compared, however, to the giant cockroaches that scurried around just about anywhere we looked—including in the bed! It was full of them.

Life in the bungalow took some getting used to. But once we did—learning to thoroughly check the bed each night before going to sleep, for example—it was fabulous.

What was not fabulous was my final paycheck. When Dr. Miller stopped by with it one day, I opened the envelope nonchalantly, looking forward to a little extra cash.

I would have to settle for pennies.

Staring at the check in disbelief, I discovered that Bob had deducted the cost of a hotel room—because, on his recommendation, I slept at the office—as well as the price of our dinner and transportation to Honolulu. The final amount of the check—which I have kept to this day—was a paltry $.08. That was my entire monetary compensation for nearly two weeks of work—not to mention enduring harassment and what very nearly became sexual assault.

Dr. Miller was almost as enraged as I was, and he urged me to complain to the Better Business Bureau. I hesitated. A young female visitor versus a local male, a member of the establishment? This was, after all, decades before #MeToo. Still, eventually convinced that with a prominent North Shore doctor at my side the case would be airtight, I took his advice and filed the complaint.

When the time came to defend himself, Bob explained he had made the mistake of hiring a bunch of "loose women" from Berkeley, which at the time was a hotbed of the sixties free-love movement. It should come as no surprise, he argued, that he wasn't the one who initiated the sexual advances—I was. When he, an unsuspecting, reputable businessman, had turned me down, he found himself unwitting victim of the wrath of a woman scorned.

In what proved to be the worst part of the ordeal, the Bureau believed him over me, the disgruntled, sex-hungry harlot out for revenge.

I felt assaulted all over again. Numb with disbelief, I

was so ashamed that I didn't tell a single soul. Meanwhile, the lessons weighed heavily on my own.

The real world was worse than I had ever imagined when, as a child, I grew up believing I had to fight to be seen and heard, to be myself. Now I learned that the fight wasn't one waged solely on the playground or within the otherwise mostly safe confines of my family. I learned that in the outside world men could not only harass, assault, and slander women, but they could get away with it. They could even further denigrate a woman who dared stand up to them. All the while, the system protected them—and they knew it.

No doubt that explained why one afternoon Bob felt emboldened to nearly run me over.

I was alone, walking home from the beach. When I heard an engine rev behind me, I turned to look. I knew the car right away.

Bob floored the gas and came at me, relishing my horror as I jumped to the side of the road as he flew past. In the aftermath, it was clear he wasn't actually trying to run me over—he genuinely could have, had that been his intention. No, he was just taking heinous delight in making me think he was, showing me he was still boss.

It was a man's world. If I wanted to succeed in it, I'd have to toughen up and fight tooth and nail. At the time it was a bitter pill to swallow; in hindsight, I realize how fortunate I was to learn the lesson when I did.

"Why now?"

My spine stiffened, dreading as I did the turn the conversation was about to take.

What felt like a lifetime after my summer in Hawaii, I was at dinner with several old friends. We were midway through a lavish meal. As fine wine flowed, the laughter got louder and the conversation more animated. Now the candlelight flickered, voices hushing as all eyes fell on the man who had just asked the question.

"Why are they complaining now?" he asked again, as though demanding an answer. "It seems no one is safe. How can they attack Charlie Rose? I mean, seriously, Charlie Rose! Who's next? Soon we won't be able to look at a Picasso without wondering if he flirted too much!"

The #MeToo movement was in full force. Knowing it was a subject that was sure to prove divisive among our group of mixed political persuasions, I had hoped to avoid it. Now it had been thrown onto the table like an extra course.

"I don't believe there's any truth to the allegations," our friend continued, a gulp of wine adding fuel to his fire. "If there were, why would they wait all these years? Why now?"

All I could think was "Me, too."

I had spoken up. I had trusted that justice would be served. Instead, I had been publicly shamed.

My friend had no idea. Why would he? He was a straight, white, affluent male.

No idea.

I had eventually moved on. So many years passed that I even forgot Bob's name. But I had held onto that check, and one day I decided to remind myself who signed it. I wanted to know what had become of him.

Bob had died in Texas five years earlier, at the age of

eighty. He was surrounded by his beloved wife of forty-one years, two sons, and three grandchildren.

Doing some quick math, I calculated that he had betrothed his beloved just two years after my summer in O'ahu; a summer in which, I was given reason to believe, I was not the only one of the eight women who found themselves forced to contend with his indiscretions. No matter. In the obituary—like when I filed my complaint against him—Bob came off as a model citizen.

I was thrilled a few years later when someone sent me an article about Bob's brief stint in jail for tax evasion. Somehow that, too, had been left out of his obituary, just one more unsavory detail conveniently overlooked.

Uneasy at the dinner table with my friends, I wondered: Why didn't I do more? Why didn't I complain to the university placement center upon my return? What about the rest of the women? Why didn't they complain? Why didn't somebody do something?

And why—almost fifty years later—do I still feel rage at the thought of that man trying to break down that door?

"Why now?" my friend demanded.

Because I guess we've finally come far enough to feel empowered to say it.

Enough.

# Breaking with the Past

The first bridge to greet me on day two in London was Westminster. Consisting of seven arches, its cast iron is painted a green recalling the leather seats in the House of Commons, the lower house of the United Kingdom's parliament. No doubt because it was designed by the same architect, the bridge features gothic detailing in the guardrail and arches. Westminster Palace, Big Ben peaking over the top of it, regally dominates the other end of the bridge.

Until it was renamed "Elizabeth Tower" in 2012, the official name of the structure known today as "Big Ben" was simply "the Clock Tower." The clock itself was formally known as "the Great Clock of Westminster." The nickname Big Ben originally applied only to the largest of the clock's five bells, "the Great Bell." Somewhere along the way the entire ensemble—tower, clock, and bells—acquired the moniker by which we know it today. As for the origin of the name itself, it's unclear, having been attributed both to Sir Benjamin Hall, who oversaw the largest bell's installation, and nineteenth-century heavyweight boxing champion "Big Ben" Benjamin Caunt.

Although designed in a neo-Gothic style suggesting a much earlier period, Westminster's Big Ben was completed comparatively recently, in 1859. 316 feet tall and forty feet on each side, the tower's decorative shields pay homage to the UK's four nations: a rose for England, a thistle for Scotland, a shamrock for Ireland, and a leek for Wales.

Turning my attention away from Big Ben and back to my stroll, I appreciated that the walkway was now separated from the road. As I felt the crisp morning air on my face, it was nice not to contend with the distraction of a constant stream of cars and buses and scooters. Instead, there were joggers and dog walkers and people heading to work. Lining the river wall, I saw tall black lampposts adorned with fish that looked as though they'd jumped right out of mythology, their scaly bodies wrapped around the bottoms of the posts. With bulging eyes and large gaping mouths they stared at passers-by. Directing my own gaze at the water, I saw a swirling, murky brown, contrasting with the whites of the boats moored in the middle of the river. Overhead a succession of leafless trees created a chaotic web between me and the sky.

Although I'd spent hours on my feet over the preceding days, my body felt good. I don't get tired walking—I never have, neither my feet, nor my legs. I get into a rhythm in which I almost feel I'm floating. It becomes effortless, as long as my body can go at its natural pace. If I'm walking with someone slow, I start to get restless—I hate to walk slowly. And I rarely need to stop.

As for my mind, it was as clear as the early-morning sky over Big Ben. Walking always does that. It creates a space in which my mind and body are free of distraction. It's a form of meditation, one which now both placed me in the present and gave my mind time to roam through the past, so I could try to see the path to a future.

That was one of the key lessons, after all, from the trek thus far: my time with Sharon and Linda, in particular, had helped me understand that I had to break with the past. Not only was I not going back to Harold, but neither would

I return to the rest of what had defined our life together. That life was gone with him. Hence my ongoing exploration of what was next.

There was, however, more to that exploration.

There was another past from which I had to break; or rather, someone else's that I was mortally afraid of repeating. It had long been a source of a deep, unrelenting anxiety, but it was made that much worse by Harold's death.

I was afraid of becoming my mother.

---

After my father's death, Mama became a mere shadow of her former self, no trace left of the strong woman I had always known her to be. Sad, lonely, insecure, she never recovered her bounce. When we took her on trips or out on the town, her sparkle would return briefly. But on her own she was never again able to muster her former vibrancy and passion. I would sign her up for classes, programs, and trips without us, but to no avail. She was lost.

She grew quiet, walking alone in the park every day. When dementia set in—or maybe it was Alzheimer's; the doctors never gave her a definitive diagnosis—she forgot her name. She forgot how to speak English. As always, she was sweet and polite to a fault, but, though still living in a house that had been home for fifty years, she ceased to inhabit our world, gradually transitioning to the next one right before our eyes.

No one seems to know what causes dementia. Genetics are believed to play a part, if not represent the single greatest contributing factor. And it's true that two of Mama's sisters had the illness. Nevertheless, I couldn't help but believe that for my mother the true cause was her deep, inescapable sorrow over my father's death.

I would never become that person. I swore it again and again, both before and after Harold got ill. What was the point of outliving him, if I didn't live fully the rest of my own life? I owed it to myself and to Harold.

I had no way of knowing whether a life lived passionately would stave off dementia. But even if I had the misfortune of sharing my mother's fate, I would do so knowing I had made the most of every moment up to my final memory. I would not give up, allowing myself to fade into the oblivion to which my mother had succumbed.

---

As Westminster Bridge retreated behind me, I passed a McDonalds with outdoor seating, followed by the enticing aroma of a bakery. Benches on raised concrete platforms now appeared along the walkway from time to time and, looking over my shoulder, I discovered that Big Ben was no longer obstructed by the palace.

A large aquarium came and went, followed by the London Dungeon—there no longer being any question that I had entered a very touristy area. As if to obliterate any remaining doubt, the London Eye—for years the world's tallest Ferris wheel—took to the sky a short distance away. Its gondolas moved, then stopped, moving and stopping again, as passengers got aboard, eager to behold views of the city only attainable from the big wheel's unparalleled heights. At its base a pier descended to the river, from which multiple boat tours were on offer.

Just beyond the London Eye, the Hungerford Bridge

and Golden Jubilee Bridges came into view. I passed a park—the first green space I'd seen in quite a while—and the wall that had been lining the river became a fence. A colorful merry-go-round brought back fond memories of the one in Golden Gate Park that I loved to ride as a child.

The bridges now directly in front of me, I took a closer look. The one in the middle—officially known as Charing Cross Bridge—was a steel truss railway structure. Two more-recent pedestrian bridges—the Golden Jubilee Bridges—shared the railway bridge's foundation piers, one on each side, supported by a series of visually striking white pylons and suspension cables, an eye-catching blend of old and new. Charing Cross railway station was on the north end of the bridge; Waterloo Station, County Hall, and the Royal Festival Hall were located on its south end.

The Golden Jubilee wasn't the only one commemorated along my walk. Signs for the Thames Path now regularly referred to the Jubilee Celebration of the River. I got out my phone and did a quick search.

It turned out the Thames Diamond Jubilee Pageant was a parade taking place just a few months later, on June 3, to celebrate sixty years since Elizabeth II had ascended to the throne. I later learned that on that day 670 boats took to the river, including the Queen herself and other members of the royal family in their own vessel. *The Guinness Book of World Records* proclaimed it the largest boat parade ever, and British media estimated that one million spectators attended in person, while more than ten million viewers watched on TV—a broadcast that lasted four and a half hours.

The boat parade would pass under the next bridge on my route, Waterloo, just over a five-minute stroll from the Hungerford Bridge and Golden Jubilee Bridges, past a succession of outdoor restaurants and a shopping mall, the Southbank Centre.

Though not nearly as interesting visually—a bland series of five unadorned, modest arches covered in dull gray stone—I would soon learn that not only it but nearby Blackfriars Bridge had sordid histories, both involving murder.

First though, after passing under Waterloo Bridge I came upon a concrete mass of geometric shapes that turned out to be nothing less than the National Theatre. I didn't know what to think. If it weren't for the signage, I might have taken it for an office or government building. Or maybe a sports facility. All I knew for sure was that I was looking at a lot of concrete.

Founded by Laurence Olivier in 1963, a who's who of well-known actors have performed in the theater's productions, which also tour theaters across the United Kingdom. As for the building itself, I wasn't the only one not quite sure what to make of it. Then Prince Charles described the monolithic edifice as "a clever way of building a nuclear power station in the middle of London without anyone objecting." Later, the building garnered the unusual distinction of appearing simultaneously on lists of the top ten most popular *and* most hated buildings in London.

Traveling back in time from the 1960s to the 1840s, I was reminded that the original Waterloo Bridge, which was much more pleasing visually but had to be replaced by the newer one in the 1940s, proved a popular place for suicide attempts. That, however, was just the beginning. In 1841, American daredevil Samuel Gilbert Scott was killed during a stunt that went horribly awry, leaving him hanging by a rope from a scaffold on the bridge. A few years later, in 1844, poet Thomas Hood wrote his famous "The Bridge of Sighs," about a young homeless woman who jumped from the bridge to her death.

Replacing the bridge did little to improve its track record. In September 1978 agents of the Bulgarian secret police, possibly with help from the KGB, assassinated dissident and outspoken critic Georgi Markov there. As though straight out of a spy movie, one reported scenario was that he had been killed with a poison pellet from an umbrella.

Not long after, nearby Blackfriars Bridge, which dates from 1869 and consists of five red wrought-iron arches ornamented with white lattice, was the scene of its own assassination. In June 1982 the body of Roberto Calvi, a former chairman of Italy's Banco Ambrosiano and known for his dealings with the Holy See, was found hanging from one of its arches. Calvi's death was initially deemed a suicide, but five bricks and $14,000 in three different currencies found in his pockets led many to believe that his was much more than a simple, self-inflicted demise.

# Bridge to Love

Days one and two had been smooth sailing. That changed on day three.

Somewhere between Blackfriars Bridge and the Millennium Bridge, the area grew confusing. The trail kept dead-ending, and I found it hard to stay near the river. The narrow passageways I ran up and down like a mouse in a maze repeatedly ended at private property, where fancy apartment buildings staked unwelcoming, no-trespassing-allowed claims to the riverbank.

Just as I was considering whether to give up on the trail, things started improving. I somehow managed to get beyond the dead ends and construction and back onto the river walkway. The buildings thinned, making way for green lawns. Coffee trucks popped up, catering to office workers who now loitered about, chatting as they drank their brew. Here and there, dogs sniffed the ground in the hopes of finding a tasty morsel, while an occasional seagull circled overhead on breezes blowing off the river.

My struggles underscored something that had occurred to me every time I found myself in an uninteresting or even unpleasant section of my walk in London. There was something powerful about expanding my sense of this city I thought I knew so well by experiencing it from its core, the good, the bad, even the occasionally ugly. It made me realize how narrow my vision of London had been until now. Exploring its heart, the artery to which it owed its very existence, deepened and broadened my understanding of it.

Not long after, I approached a pedestrian bridge, the Millennium Bridge, which arched over the walkway and spanned the river, ending at the Tate Modern Museum of Art. I was reassured to observe the bridge did not appear to be wobbling.

That's because when it opened in June of 2000, pedestrians were alarmed to feel it sway beneath them. The swaying proved so bad that not only was the bridge nicknamed the "Wobbly Bridge," but it was closed that very same day. A couple of days later it was closed indefinitely to rectify serious structural issues. The ensuing reparations took nearly two years.

The issues were attributed to an unconscious tendency of pedestrians crossing a bridge to match their footsteps to the lateral sway—unknowingly exacerbating it. The phenomenon is so well known that nearby Albert Bridge has a sign dating from 1873 warning marching soldiers to break step when crossing. I could only assume that the architects of the Millennium Bridge had neither been in the army nor, therefore, done much marching over bridges with lateral sway. Lesson learned.

Confident that I could cross the footbridge without incident, I climbed the stairs up from the river walk, welcomed by the south façade of Saint Paul's Cathedral. Situated on the highest point in London, throughout the city the church's majestic seventeenth-century dome is hard to miss. In fact, until 1963 no other building in London was taller. The cathedral itself was erected on the site of an original church built in 604, and, relatively more recently, made its way into the homes of hundreds of millions of people the world over when Prince Charles and Princess Diana were married there.

The start of one marriage returning me to the start of another, a flashback.

Harold and I were sharing a house, beginning to believe we were destined to be together, that a new life was possible if we could exorcise our personal demons. While I had been burned at the altar once before, he had failed to create the happy family life he had dreamt of for his two children. Could taking the risk of committing our lives to one another possibly get us beyond our past traumas?

It was a morning I'll never forget. We were backing out of the garage, continuing some debate or another started over breakfast. Exasperated, Harold slammed on the brakes, turned to me, and exclaimed "All right, damn it, let's just get married!"

I'm not sure who was more shocked. We stared at each other in silence—until one of us, and then the other, started laughing. We laughed until we cried, releasing untold amounts of pent-up tension.

Unlike Charles and Di, we never looked back. Once we committed, it was as if all the issues keeping us apart turned to dust, swept away by the wind.

Now subjected to cool gusts of it, I crossed the no-longer-wobbly bridge, bringing another London landmark into view: the Tate Modern.

Like the Battersea Power Station I had passed on day one of my London walk, the Tate Modern had originally been a power station; specifically, the Bankside Power Station. What's more, both were designed by the same architect. Unlike its four-stacked counterpart upstream, however, the Tate only has one smokestack, a large, imposing column dominating the façade and rising high above the rest of the structure. On either side of it, three sets of long, narrow windows break up the museum's otherwise simple brick face.

As I approached the Tate now, I observed children skateboarding and couples walking arm-in-arm. Finding my way inside, I headed for Turbine Hall, a vast space used for large-scale sculpture and installation art. Eighty-five feet tall and five hundred feet long, with a roof consisting of 524 glass panes, even if it were devoid of art the space would impress, a tour de force in its own right.

As it turned out, at the moment I was in fact much less interested in art than I was in a bite to eat. I headed for the museum café, where I had a mouthwatering quiche lorraine with caramelized onion chutney and a glass of red wine. After the meal, content with the relaxed atmosphere, as well as the view of the Thames and the skyline, I decided to prolong my stay with a cappuccino. I savored its rich aroma and the warmth of it in my hands, grateful for the sort of luxury that had often been hard to come by during our pastoral walk the previous week.

Not long after reluctantly leaving behind the Tate, I came upon London Bridge, disappointed when reminded that the boring, modern bridge I now saw was not the cantilevered one we visualized as children when singing "London Bridge is Falling Down."

As for exactly which bridge that nursery rhyme might have referred to, it's hard to say. The current bridge replaced a nineteenth-century one that, though not exactly "falling down," had in fact been sinking, which resulted in its being dismantled and shipped off for a second life in Arizona, of all places. Still, the nursery rhyme dated to much earlier, to the seventeenth century. Back then, London Bridge was a medieval stone structure that spanned the river for 600 years. It had followed a succession of wooden bridges, including the very first bridge of them all, built by the Roman founders of London.

The location of London Bridge, after all, was of supreme importance. Until a bridge was built there, London did not exist. Once one was constructed, a small trading and shipping settlement on the north side grew into the town of Londinium, complemented by a smaller settlement at the southern end of the bridge. Londinium eventually became the capital of Roman Britain.

As I now followed the walkway in and out of galleries created by buildings built at the river's edge, I came upon Hay's Galleria. Twin five-story, light-colored brick buildings dating to the 1800s, they were joined by a giant wrought-iron-and-glass roof modelled on Milan's Galleria on the Piazza del Duomo. I paused to admire the stunning architecture, my neck straining as I looked toward the sky, varying hues of blue and white and gray visible through the glass.

Named after the owner of the brewhouse on the site in the 1600s, in 1856 the complex was converted into an enclosed dock called Hay's Wharf. At its peak, eighty percent of the dry produce imported to London passed through the wharf, as the result of which it earned the moniker "the Larder of London."

Having no need of dry goods, I continued on my way, the river soon dominated by the HMS Belfast, a large naval warship moored in this very spot since 1971. Commissioned shortly before the outbreak of World War II, initially the ship was part of the British naval blockade against Germany. Much later, it took part in the Normandy landings, as well as many subsequent overseas commissions, including combat in the Korean War. These days the only action the ship sees are the hundreds of thousands of tourists to which it annually plays host.

As I passed the Belfast's ticket office, just up ahead the Tower Bridge came into full view. *This*, I thought, *is a masterpiece, a true work of art.*

Despite being constructed in the late 1800s, the bridge was designed in a much earlier Gothic style intended to complement the Tower of London, its turrets visible on the opposite shore. As I approached, the bridge glowed in the sun, its two magnificent stone towers a beautiful caramel color. In stark contrast, the cityscape acting as backdrop had been overtaken by menacing dark clouds, making the bridge that much more radiant.

Wending my way through increasingly dense crowds of tourists loitering about as if it were the first day of summer as opposed to the end of February—including two newlyweds in wedding attire, photographers in tow—I marveled at the towers. Each had four turrets and six stories of windows framed in a lighter stone, with steeply pitched slate roofs. The towers looked as though they could have been lifted from a medieval castle, now controlling access to a navigable river instead of a defensive moat.

A drawbridge between the two towers allows passage to important port facilities between London Bridge and the Tower of London. On either side of the towers, suspension spans connect the bridge with the banks of the river. 40,000 vehicles cross the bridge daily, not to mention countless pedestrians.

Still enraptured by the contrast between the glowing bridge and the foreboding sky, I couldn't resist capturing the moment with my iPhone. In the weeks ahead I would often present the picture as evidence that the weather in London had been beautiful, even though all that people back home heard about Europe were the awful winter storms.

I took a seat on a nearby lawn and ate an orange, relishing its invigorating citrus scent and a glorious patch of sunshine, as well as the activity around me. And then, as I watched the wedding couple pose for photos, I found myself transported back in time to another bridge; specifically, a bridge in Pittsburg thirty years before.

In 1977 I was product manager of Control Data's super-computer business. The environment was as cutthroat as it got. I learned to swear like a longshoreman, make my opinions known, and hold my ground. Despite being more like a bull in a china shop than a savvy consensus builder, I was able to convince my bosses that I merited a key role in the organization.

In that environment, any weakness—real or perceived—could be used against you. What was used against me was my status as a "techie," since I had come into management through the technical side of the organization. This was seen as a shortcoming by a new group of hotshot execs who disagreed with the notion that technology was the answer to our problems. When I found myself blocked at every turn, I realized I had to fight on their turf—I needed the skills and credibility afforded by an MBA.

I was accepted to Harvard and Stanford business schools, as well as awarded generous fellowships. But as I was debating which one to attend, things took a very unexpected turn.

"Would you like to be marketing manager for the computer business?" my boss asked, leaving me stunned. Competent and collaborative, with the slight paunch typical of a middle-aged father and glasses typical of businessmen who spend long hours crunching numbers, he had popped into my office unannounced. Eyes wide, smile broad, he sat on the edge of his seat on the other side of my desk, anticipating my reaction.

"The *entire* computer business?" I asked. My heart was racing, and I was holding my breath, afraid to exhale until I was sure I'd heard right. A phone rang in the office next door, followed by muffled conversation.

"The *entire* computer business," he laughed, before sharing the details.

It was an executive position. Eighty people would report to me. I would report to the global head of Sales and Marketing.

The choice was much easier than which school to attend. In fact, from one moment to the next, there wasn't any choice at all. Suddenly it made little sense to pursue an MBA, since the whole purpose for bothering to spend the two years it would take was to position myself for an opportunity like this one. Even with an MBA it wasn't a sure thing. Now, without one, it had fallen into my lap.

I turned down the two best business schools in the country and took the job.

A few days later, I was in for another surprise. The

company CFO, Bill Fitzgerald, asked for an unscheduled meeting. Another middle-aged executive, with gray temples and eyes as focused when sizing up a person as when scrutinizing a spreadsheet, he and I had always found common ground in our shared love of numbers.

"Tania," he said, as I walked into his large, luminous office and took a seat on a leather chair, "I have some good news, and I have some bad news."

"Yes?" I asked calmly, as though alarm bells weren't sounding throughout my body, my palms suddenly sweaty.

"The good news," he began, his delivery calm and cool, "is that your division has been transferred to me."

That was in fact good news. I liked working with Bill.

"The bad news…" He hesitated, as though getting up his nerve. "The bad news is that the division has been renamed, and some of your new team has been transferred to Sales."

"How much of my new team?"

Bill look down at his desk and sighed.

"Seventy-seven of them," he said.

"Seventy—what?"

A silence descended between us. Once again I was stunned, this time for all the wrong reasons.

"They considered sending you back to California to head up development," Bill offered, trying to soften the blow. "But they couldn't imagine asking managers who were three levels your senior when you started to report to you now."

He hoped I could understand.

It wasn't until recently that I truly did. It was simple: at that time, executives were not about to let a woman manage other high-level executives and market leaders. It would have been too big a shock—the men would have found it intolerable. A woman! And a young woman at that! Not a chance. There would have been riots in the cubicles.

I wondered how the original decision had ever gotten approved. I imagined a poor soul being carried off to the guillotine in the middle of the night, his head rolling as higher-ups issued panicked evacuation orders for what was to have been my group.

Whatever the case, one thing was certain: I had passed up Stanford and Harvard for a job where I managed a mere three people.

When I was first promoted to management, my father had given me a chilling warning: "Don't put your head up." I now saw that, in a sense, he was right. Rising above the fray, standing out and getting noticed, was sometimes a double-edged sword. All the same, while I had compassion for how being exiled twice and feeling perpetually disempowered and out of place could leave him terrified of life—would they come for him a third time?—I would draw different lessons from my misfortunes. I would not allow others to hold me back.

It wasn't long before I reapplied and got into Stanford again, this time into an executive program that took one year instead of the usual two. Yet again, however, there was a catch: I had to be sponsored by my company, but my company didn't want to sponsor me.

"We don't want to set a precedent," the head of Human Resources told me, for what felt like the hundredth time. His voice on the other end of the phone was devoid of emotion, as though he were reading from a script; as though he couldn't be bothered to seriously consider the sponsorship; as though, if he did, scores of mid-career managers were sure to flock to the top schools in the country for a business education.

After weeks of no progress, it occurred to me to take a new approach. I called Stanford and asked if anyone associated with my firm had ever attended.

"Why yes," the woman said, "a man called Harold Hahn from Commercial Credit was here just last year."

Commercial Credit was a finance subsidiary of my company, based in Baltimore. I looked up Harold in the interoffice directory and called his number.

"Mr. Hahn's office," a woman answered. "How may I help you?"

"My name is Tania Romanov, and I'd like to speak to Mr. Hahn, please."

"I'm sorry, dear, that's not possible. He's not here anymore." The woman sounded more like an endearing grandmother than a busy executive secretary.

"I need to talk to him. Can you tell me where he's moved?"

"He went to Stanford, and now he has taken a position with Control Data, in Minneapolis."

"I'm in Minneapolis. Could you tell me which office he's in?"

"No, I'm afraid not, dear. I don't know."

"Do you have a phone number for him?"

"I don't, honey. I don't think he has one yet."

"Well, can I leave a message with you to ask him to call me?"

"Certainly, I can put it with the rest of his mail. No problem."

As I was about to thank the woman and wrap up the conversation, a light bulb went off.

"Actually, ma'am, could you please tell me where you send his mail?"

"I just put it in a big yellow interoffice envelope and mark it with those letters they gave me."

"Right. And what are those letters?"

"Just a minute, let me see . . . Here it is. It's HQN10Q."

"H-Q-N-1-0-Q?" I repeated.

"Yes, dear. I know it seems odd, but it does get to him."

"Is he tall?"

"Oh yes, Mr. Hahn is very tall."

"Thank you so much—I think I know where to find him."

The initials stood for: HQ, headquarters; N, north wing; 10, tenth floor; and Q, the office number. I knew because I was in HQN10R, just two doors down from the tall new guy managing troubled projects for the president.

It didn't take me long to meet the new guy. Unfortunately, he couldn't help me either.

"I've only been here a short time," he explained, when our paths crossed in the hall, "but I've already had a run-in with one of the old-guard executives. He told me not to let Stanford go to my head. He said that here an MBA and a dime might get you a cup of coffee—but not much more! I'm sorry, but I don't think I can help you."

I hated to admit it, but he was probably right.

"Why do you want to go to business school anyway?" he asked, stepping aside as a frazzled secretary raced by with a pile of papers. Phones rang in the background.

I was so tired of the question that I came up with an answer sure to disarm anyone who asked it: "I want to be president of the company."

"You?" Harold exclaimed, not even bothering to hide his disbelief. He was lucky I didn't cut his head off. I probably would have, if it hadn't been so high up.

We were not off to an auspicious start. All the same, we didn't work together and, after he moved to a different floor, for a while our paths rarely crossed.

I had just about given up on the Stanford idea when an executive management meeting was called to discuss an increasingly important issue: affirmative action. In a large room full of suits—which included just one other woman and one Black man—the president of the company, doing his best to affect genuine enthusiasm, explained the importance of fairness in our policies and the need to promote women and minorities. At the end, his mouth as dry as his delivery had been, he asked if there were any questions.

I didn't miss a beat.

"If we're interested in developing more female executives, would we consider sponsoring one to go to Stanford Business School?"

A bunch of heads turned my direction. My gaze fixed on the head of HR, a pale, portly, passionless bureaucrat, I pretended not to notice.

"See me later on that, all right?" the president replied.

"Sure," I said, looking his way and trying not to sound eager. But inside I felt the devious satisfaction of someone who has at long last backed their opponent into a corner.

When the meeting ended, I made a beeline for the president. The head of HR was even quicker, already making the familiar case against "precedent." No matter. I had lost multiple battles but finally won the war. I got my sponsorship to Stanford.

A couple of years later, my master's degree hanging in

my office, I was a vice president in charge of assessing the viability of existing lines of business and recommending new investments.

Harold, still a casual acquaintance at the time, was running a number of troubled divisions spread throughout the world. He was good at getting businesses back on track and deciding how to divest, if necessary.

We were in a staff meeting with the company president. As Harold briefed the team on a nuclear valve company in Pittsburgh, he heard the words every line manager dreads: "Why don't you bring out a financial expert from corporate?"

Getting "help from corporate" was almost always a prelude to bad news.

"I think Tania could work with you," the president continued, oblivious as both Harold and I cringed. "We really need to make progress on stemming these losses."

I was about as excited to go to Pittsburgh as Harold was to get my team's help; which is to say, not at all. At the time, warranted or not, my limited knowledge of Pittsburgh suggested it was little more than a polluted postindustrial nightmare of abandoned factories. I didn't know anything about nuclear valves, but I found it hard to imagine they were of any strategic importance to the company's future. Besides, I needed to focus all my attention on struggles with the computer business.

The decision was not mine to make. Consequently, my financial man, Singh, and I joined Harold and his own financial guru, Allan, on a trip to Pittsburgh.

It was March. I assumed the weather would be cold and gray. It exceeded my expectations—it was even colder and grayer. Harold offered me a ride from the hotel to the office.

"You really don't want to be here, do you?" he commented, as we turned out of the parking lot.

"Well, this unit is bleeding cash, and there are better ways to invest the company's money. The computer business is in a critical stage right now."

Without responding, Harold peered into his rearview mirror and merged onto the highway.

"I'd really like it if you went into this with an open mind," he commented, after a moment of reflection.

"You're right. I owe you and the business at least that much," I agreed, my stance softening. "What are some of your ideas about how to move forward?"

"My team has some proposals. I'm not sure how solid they are, but everyone knows it's down to the wire. I don't want you to cut them off at the feet when they present what they've come up with."

"Why would I do that?"

"My staff is terrified of you! They sweat bullets before going into sessions with your team."

I laughed. The night before we'd had a long meeting about a water purification company in Holland. It hadn't even occurred to me that his guys might secretly be quaking in their boots. Everyone had seemed calm enough to me. Now I suspected they didn't want to lose face by having a woman shoot holes in their plan.

"I've tried to convince them that your tough guy approach is probably just an act, so you get taken seriously—that underneath it all you're actually a reasonable person. They just look at me like I'm crazy."

"Imagine if they had to deal with me before I left that chip on my shoulder back at Stanford!"

I was referring to a comment our HR guy had made, his passive-aggressive way of begrudgingly acknowledging that my relentlessness had paid off and earned me a seat at the table. At Stanford I had learned enough about power trips to laugh it off and pretend it was a compliment.

"I couldn't believe it when he said that," Harold replied. "He would never dare say something like that to me. I can see that our world looks a lot different when you're the only woman."

He had no idea. But I appreciated the sentiment.

"As far as this beleaguered group is concerned," he continued, "we're the ones with the power to close them down. So, it would be good if we looked like we were all on the same page."

I had never worked with Harold. I was pleasantly surprised to discover that not only did he have a mind well-suited to working on the seemingly intractable problems we had come to address, but he was a caring human being, as well. I was also impressed that he had managed to bring me around to his way of seeing things before we engaged with the team.

We spent a long day in meetings, where it was made abundantly clear that the on-site team had no interest in being an unappreciated stepchild of a computer company. That being the case, we successfully developed some alternative paths forward, including preparing the division to be sold to another company where it would be a better fit.

At the end of a productive day, Allan, Singh, Harold, and I headed to dinner.

As part of an effort to revitalize the city, the old Pittsburg train station had been converted into shops and restaurants, complete with a pedestrian bridge over the

Monongahela River, connecting our hotel to the station. We crossed the bridge and had a long meal at a lively Italian restaurant. Over pasta and chianti, Allan and Singh discussed financial details, while Harold and I found we had much common ground to explore, including our experiences at Stanford. We knew the same professors and had a seemingly endless list of anecdotes to share, laughing and reminiscing as we revisited our respective graduate school experiences.

All the while, in the back of my mind, there was a particular anecdote that I could have shared but didn't; one that was in fact no laughing matter. Far from it, it had proved to be a pivotal moment marking a definitive before and after in my life.

I went to Stanford because, as a techie, I wasn't good enough. The guys with the MBAs had something I didn't. Just like once upon a time on a playground, I had to prove myself worthy of being among their ranks.

One day I was in a class of forty executives, the youngest in the room and one of only three women. In response to something I said—I no longer recall what it was—in front of everyone the professor asked, "What are you trying to prove?"

"I'm as good as you guys are," I responded reflexively, my insecurity laid bare.

A collective gasp was followed by absolute silence. I wasn't the only one stopped dead in her tracks, waiting with bated breath for whatever came next.

"You're not as good as we are," the professor countered, measuring his words, not so much as a hint of irony in his tone. "You're better."

And that was the end of it.

I no longer felt the need to fight to be seen or heard or taken seriously for who I was. It was as if the professor had given me permission to let go of that misguided image of myself, of the perceived need to wage an endless fight, its roots reaching all the way back to my embattled childhood. I no longer had anything to prove. I had become the person I strived to be when, as a teenager, it seemed the whole world was against me.

My conversation with Harold eventually ventured into more personal territory. He explained that he was not only an avid skier, but a hiker training to climb Mt. Rainier. Later, he divulged he was separated from his wife and figuring out how to manage shared custody of two young children. By the time dinner was over, rather than the adversarial business partner I had met originally, he now felt almost like an old friend.

The four of us spent some time exploring the station, which *The New Yorker* once proclaimed, "one of the great pieces of Beaux-Arts architecture in America." A single look at the building's rotunda, and it was easy to see why. Originally used as a place for passengers to arrive and depart in carriages, the vaulted enclosure was made of brown terra cotta, with three elegant arches and regal turrets on each corner. Its floor was paved in brick, and the four cities served by the Pennsylvania Railroad were inscribed within its walls: Pittsburgh, New York, Philadelphia, and Washington. The rotunda itself was such an architectural treasure that it had been included in the National Register of Historic Places before the rest of the station, which wasn't added until three years later.

When the time came to head back over the bridge, Harold and I sauntered behind our two colleagues, as if we didn't want the evening to end.

We didn't.

Far from it, in the middle of that bridge, somehow we fell in love.

We didn't touch. We didn't say a word. As our finance guys—deep in conversation—ambled toward the hotel, we simply paused, looked into each other's eyes, and knew.

Pittsburgh wasn't such a bad place after all.

It's held a very special place in my heart ever since.

---

The next day the four of us returned to the office for more meetings. Late afternoon, we headed to the airport to fly back to Minneapolis. Having checked in early and arrived at the gate before it opened, we decided to split up. Allan and Singh needed to do more work on the financials, while Harold and I had other business to discuss. We opted to do it over a drink—and ended up talking about just about everything other than business.

An hour later our group reconvened at the gate and boarded the plane. Since this was a last-minute trip, none of us had seats together. The plane was nearly full.

As it pulled back from the gate, the man next to me asked, "And what brings you to Rochester?"

"I'm not going to Rochester," I replied, "I am heading home to Minneapolis."

Rochester, Minnesota, was only sixty-five miles from Minneapolis. Still, I wasn't sure why he assumed that was my destination.

"Minneapolis?"

"Uh huh. And what about you? Are you heading to

the Mayo Clinic?" That was the biggest draw in Rochester.

"No, I'm heading *home*," he insisted, as if I were slow. "The Mayo Clinic is in Minnesota."

Something wasn't right. It took me a second, then I got it: my new friend thought he was on a flight to Rochester, New York—not Minnesota.

I pushed the stewardess button.

"Yes?" she asked, in the hurried tone of someone who needs to take their seat.

"Where are we going?" I blurted out, a surge of panic rushing through my body as the plane began pulling back from the gate.

"*Where are we going?*" she repeated, her own expression overcome with concern. "Rochester, of course. Where are *you* going?"

"Stop the plane!" I called out, pulling my boarding pass from the seat pocket and holding it up. "We're going to Minneapolis!"

In today's post-9/11 days of heightened security, it's hard to imagine how four people could possibly end up on the wrong plane, never mind each find seats on it—but that was exactly what had happened. While we were strolling around the airport, our gate had been reassigned to the flight to Rochester, New York. The plane we were supposed to be on was now leaving from a different gate. We hadn't heard the announcement.

A panicked call was made to the cockpit, and soon we were taxiing back to the terminal. The plane to Minnesota did the same, and all was well.

Better than well, actually.

On our new, correct flight Harold and I were upgraded to first class. The stewardess asked what we wanted to drink. I had a question of my own.

"So where do we go from here?" I asked, turning to Harold.

We spent the entire trip back figuring out what our life together was going to look like. Harold was separated but not yet divorced. Working out the separation was painful, and leaving his ideal notion of a nuclear family with two small children was killing him. Now suddenly I was in the mix.

It wasn't exactly going to be easy for me, either.

But the two of us had fallen hard.

# Lunch

Day four was not one to write home about. After spending much of it again struggling to navigate the river walk, which was frequently overtaken by construction projects that made it hard to proceed, I eventually ended up in Greenwich. Given how hard I had worked to get there, I had hoped for a bigger payoff.

At least the pubs along the way had amusing and imaginative names: The Dog and Bell, The Harp of Erin, The Orange Bull. But many were closed. The open ones were mostly deserted.

As for Greenwich itself, it was the antithesis of Oxford. All kinds of "ye olde" shops lined the streets, which were overrun with tourists. Little of what I saw had anything in common with the charming, authentic towns Sharon, Linda, and I had visited at the beginning of our journey. I was reminded of Thomas Kinkade's saccharine sweet, overly sentimental paintings, their surreal colors and idealized settings evoking a romanticized past.

Ironic, given that the town was a global reference point, the home of Greenwich Mean Time, the standard by which the whole world—which ordinarily agrees on so little—at least agrees on what time it is.

Presently, it was lunchtime. None of the restaurants appealed, so I ended up getting prepared food at a Marks and Spencer. As I had on previous trips, I wished "Marks & Sparks," as it is affectionately known, would enter the US market. When I first visited England in 1968 and decried its food the worst I had ever encountered, never could I have imagined that the quality of the prepared foods in their grocery stores would make such leaps and bounds. I couldn't help but think some of the chains could even teach Whole Foods a thing or two.

Lunch in tow, I walked the short distance to the National Maritime Museum, admiring its vast, green grounds—200 acres of them, in fact—as gravel crunched under my feet. The main building, painted a warm rose color and featuring a distinctive, classical portico, was set back a considerable distance from the street, flanked by two large wings. I suspected the complex might have originally been a palace, but later learned it was previously the Royal Hospital School.

As its name suggests, the museum highlights Britain's maritime history. Its holdings include art, cartography, manuscripts, ship models, and navigational, astronomical, and chronological instruments.

As I sat on a bench eating my sandwich, I considered the entrance more closely. Crowned at its highest point by a seashell, the façade's entablature was topped by two fanciful boats that appeared to be galleys, given that they had not only sails but also oars. Between the boats, two mythological sea creatures, each with tails, one with the face of a man, the other with the head of a lion, embraced a coat of arms featuring four anchors. On the ground, under the watchful eye of a bearded face I could only assume was Poseidon, two giant, real-life anchors ensured the building wasn't carried off by the sea.

As I watched groups of school kids stream in and out of the museum, I couldn't help but think it would be fun to bring Beth and Brad and their families here. That, in turn, got me thinking about when Beth and her husband Sloan flew to meet Harold and me in the Dolomites.

At the time Harold and I were tackling increasingly difficult climbs, but the kids were in a whole different league: they were serious mountain climbers who loved a challenge.

Somewhere during our trek, we parted ways. The kids headed off to a *via ferrata*, one of the cabled ascents laid out by the army during World War I. Harold and I took a longer but safer route to our overnight spot high atop a mountain.

When Harold and I reached an overlook, we were stunned to see Beth and Sloan on the side of a distant cliff.

"I can't bear to watch," Harold said. "Let's keep going."

It wasn't just Beth and Sloan he was worried about. Beth was more than five months pregnant; our first granddaughter was scaling that cliff, too.

Thinking of being in the mountains with Beth reminded me of the countless New Year's Eves we celebrated in remote huts in the Colorado Rockies, part of the tenth mountain division hut system built during World War II.

Not for us a simple party with balloons and horns. Harold and I would come home from work in San Francisco, get on a late plane to Denver, then drive to Vail to join our friends. Early the next morning we would set out for the chosen trail, cross country skiing with backpacks into some remote hut with wood-burning stove and bunk beds. The first years we carried everything in our packs; over time we learned to tow the food and champagne on a sled.

Our crazy-clean German friend Helga would insist on cleaning the entire hut before we got settled. Each night another friend, Bob, would snore so loudly no one could sleep. I would be so sick from the altitude it would be days before my headache went away.

None of that mattered.

Alone in the wilderness, making fresh tracks, skiing and snowshoeing, we had such fun. One of my fondest memories is from the middle of one particular freezing night. As I climbed to the bathroom atop an old water tower next to a nineteenth-century train station, I was awestruck by a full moon, an infinitude of silvery stars, and the sight of white peaks in all directions. I didn't care about my cold butt. All that mattered was the glory of the moment, just me and that high-altitude beauty, literally taking my breath away.

Eventually Beth and Brad got old enough to realize their parents' alpine adventures were way more exciting than their run-of-the-mill parties. Soon they joined us, as did our friends' kids. Each year the group grew, until only the largest huts were big enough for our needs.

As for my needs, my immediate ones had now been met. I ended my visit to Greenwich by confirming there were water taxies to and from central London. The next day, Sharon, Graham, and I would start our final day's walk here, ending at the Thames Barrier.

# The Thames Barrier

Day five, the final day, began downstairs in my hotel, where I was delighted to reunite with Sharon and Graham. Though dressed in casual wear suitable for walking, Sharon had reclaimed the well-put-together look—coiffed hair, light make-up, energetic glow—that had gradually faded during our walk in the countryside, when we carried only the barest essentials, laundered our clothes in the sink, and showed up to luxury hotels looking as though we'd been playing in mud.

After a quick coffee and much animated conversation, as though rather than mere days we hadn't seen each other for months, we headed for the Tube.

A ten-minute ride, and we found ourselves a short distance from Westminster Pier. Big Ben once again looking over our shoulder and, across the river, the London Eye keeping its own tabs on us, we were soon aboard a ferry to Greenwich.

The wind in our faces, the open sky overhead, it felt good to be on the water. Funny that after so many days following the river, this was the first time we had actually been on it. Its left bank and its right, on bridges over it time and time again, but not actually on it until now.

As Graham, Sharon, and I chatted, I appreciated yet another novel perspective on the city, one only possible from the water. We were in the middle of everything, on the city's main artery, yet the empty space between us and the banks gave the illusion of being somehow detached from it all, objective observers watching from a safe distance. We could have gone inside the boat, but I liked being on the upper deck, having an unfiltered view of the scenery, so much of which was familiar.

We passed the pile of concrete known as the Royal National Theatre, the Millennium Bridge, and the Tate Modern. Shakespeare's Globe Theatre came and went, as did the Shard—at seventy-two stories, the tallest building in the UK—the Tower Bridge, and the Tower of London. After Canary Wharf, Greenwich Park, and the Royal Observatory, we came to the final stop, which also happened to be ours: Greenwich Pier.

Though excited as we stepped off the boat and headed east, our enthusiasm soon waned. Rather than a picturesque or intellectually stimulating build-up to the grand finale of our adventure, we were disappointed to discover this segment of the trail was mostly a dull and drab mix of industry and housing and abandoned properties.

That all changed when we eventually made it to our destination, the Thames Barrier.

A breeze in our hair and a saltiness teasing our tongues, a smell that might have been fish or seaweed or something else altogether filled our noses. Before us, a succession of seven massive, bonnet-shaped structures clad in shiny metal tiles. No matter that they'd been there since the early eighties; they still looked futuristic, the only hint as to their function being their strategic placement across the width of the river.

What we now beheld was nothing less than an engineering marvel; more specifically, a series of retractable floodgates essential to London's very survival. The city sits in a floodplain, rendering it vulnerable to unusually high tides and North Sea storm surges. When necessary, the barrier is raised to hold back the sea and prevent the Thames from overspilling its banks.

The risk is more real with each passing year. Storm surges coinciding with high spring tides can result in surges of up to nearly twelve feet, with the potential to flood forty-five square miles of land. Needless to say, the implications to London would be devastating.

"It's so impressive," I commented, trying to let sink in the monumental importance of the silver bonnets, not to mention the almost inconceivable notion that they were somehow capable of holding back the sea.

"It is," Graham concurred. "I just wonder what they're going to do next."

"Do next?" Sharon asked, brushing the hair out of her eyes.

"The Barrier was only designed to be operational through 2030—which is obviously just a few years from now."

"Really?" I asked, alarmed. "So then what?" I looked to the right of the Barrier. The churning seawater suddenly seemed much more menacing than just a moment before.

"The engineers say it will actually hold up a lot longer than 2030—hopefully a few more decades—but still…the way things are going with the climate, I hope it's not wishful thinking."

So did I. It was hard to imagine how something that looked like an art installation could hold back the North Sea in a winter roar, how it could possibly withstand all we were throwing at it, between melting ice caps and the increasing radicalization of climate patterns.

Putting out of my mind the possibility that the Barrier might one day fail, I marveled at how the sun reflected off the gates' distinctive metallic curves. Losing myself still more in what I saw before me, I found myself trying to capture it with the camera on my cell. I could almost feel the power of the river surging through the majestic gates, those burnished ovals soaring out of the water like birds taking to flight.

It occurred to me that this—and not Greenwich—was the marvel to which people should be flocking. Greenwich Mean Time was set hundreds of years ago; it already had its day. Now was the Barrier's time to shine. It was here that lessons of the twenty-first century, the very real threat of climate change, could be appreciated firsthand. Here was a museum that school kids needed to visit, one that explained how to prepare for catastrophe, that illustrated the threats faced by low-lying islands without protections from rising sea levels.

But no.

This spot was deserted. And not only by tourists; there was nobody here at all, no one other than us. That included the restaurant where we had hoped to have lunch. It, too, was desolate.

When the time came to go, instead of a heartfelt celebration of our accomplishment, we exchanged hugs that felt a little hollow. After one last picture, we turned to leave.

That's when we realized we didn't know how. We weren't going back the way we came; instead, after finding someplace to have lunch, we hoped to go back to London on the Tube. Easier said than done.

We wandered through an area of abandoned warehouses and empty lots, of cracked pavement and random sections of chain-link fence. After coming to several dead ends, we neared a busy road, our path to freedom once again obstructed by metal fencing. I started to climb over it, but was stopped by barbed wire.

Frustrated but driven by our rumbling bellies, we persisted, eventually finding our way out of the post-industrial labyrinth and to the pub on the other side of the road. Imagine our disappointment, however, when after all the effort we'd made to get there, we learned that the restaurant had finished serving lunch.

It took some pleading, but the server took pity on us. Soon we were wolfing down fish and chips, gratefully quenching our thirst with some beers. We needed the calories. And not only to replenish those we had spent, but because we still had a long walk through another semi-industrial area to get to the bus that would take us to the Underground.

Although—other than the Barrier itself—our last day had proven anticlimactic, we put on a smile and made the best of it. Wasn't it enough that we were together, that we'd been blessed with good weather, and that, last but far from least, we had arrived at our goal?

Like with Linda, I didn't know when I would see Sharon again. All three of us, however, would stay in touch, our time together having forged an enduring bond. There would be monthly calls, as well as visits whenever and wherever circumstances allowed. Sharon would indeed leave behind the corporate world and embrace a creative path, founding a not-for-profit that makes theater more accessible for young people. Linda would scale back her involvement on boards, successfully leading and selling a startup, enabling her to settle into a comfortable life. Through it all, we would continue to support one another, forever grateful for our transformative time together on the Thames.

---

The Underground ride back was a long one. After Sharon and Graham changed lines to head to their apartment, I was left alone with my thoughts.

Although at first I tried to reflect on how the trip had affected me, all I could think about instead was that it represented the longest walk in many years I'd done without Harold. Rather than a sense of accomplishment, I felt empty.

It also bothered me that this wonderful walk, my first adventure after Harold's death, had ended with a fizzle. Were we just too hard an act to follow?

An unexpected chuckle escaped me. Whether or not *we* were a hard act to follow, there was no doubt that following *him* had never been easy.

We both loved biking. With his long legs, Harold was stronger and faster and would go ahead, leaving me trailing somewhere behind. In and of itself, that didn't bother me—but I wasn't about to give up having a say in where we went. So, I bought a whistle and hung it around my neck. If Harold took a turn I didn't like, I blew my whistle until he stopped. Once I caught up, we would discuss which route to take.

He found it in turns hysterically funny, outrageously annoying, and, most telling of all, the model he wanted for a marriage. It didn't matter who was bigger or stronger or out in front—the other person was going to be heard. Or, as he liked to tease, "Tania knows how to lead even from behind."

Lulled deeper into relaxation by the rhythm of the train, I recalled his sixtieth birthday, when I surprised him with a helicopter ski adventure in British Columbia—a trip on which I would have no need of my whistle. When I broke my ACL on the first descent, the helicopter carried me off to safety.

Free to choose his own routes, Harold enjoyed the day, while I got help at the medical clinic. Since I was an "older woman"—I was barely 50—the doctor explained, I would no longer be very active. Although I probably wouldn't need surgery, he added, I would have to "be careful."

I chose to have the surgery and obsessively followed a six-month recovery program. That fall Harold and I were off on a major trek through Bhutan. A nasty tumble might have prevented me from following him down Mt. Whistler, but there was no way I was going to miss Bhutan—no matter the Canadian doctor's highly suspect advice.

# Bhutan

Our Bhutan trek would forever remain a highlight of our lives.

Harold and I spent twenty-three days deep in the Himalayas, including a week at a 14,000-foot plateau next to Tibet, as well as crossing multiple passes approaching 18,000 feet.

I loved the Himalayas. We were experienced trekkers. I was in my element.

The demands and distractions of my day-to-day left behind, modern life receded in this remote country. There were no high-rises or fast food. There were few factories. By law, the people of Bhutan still wore traditional dress, the women in long, narrow wool skirts, the men in *gohs*—robes wrapped to knee length—even on the trek.

But as we drove deeper into the countryside, I started noticing something discomfiting, something that appeared glaringly out of place in this seemingly circumspect society.

Penises.

Could it really be?

Our vehicle pulled into the last town before the trek. From there, we walked through villages unreachable by car.

Even here, every house had penises painted on them. And these were not small or subtle renderings. These were giant, golden, erect specimens, some pointing up, some facing down. The latter often had huge testicles on top, with glorious hairy crowns. Prayer flags and penises somehow cohabited seamlessly, oblivious to any possible irony.

Unable to hold back any longer, I asked our guide, Tandin, a young man on break from school in Darjeeling.

"Why are there penises painted on the side of that house?"

Tandin had a long, narrow face with chiseled features. I could easily imagine him striding a Mongolian plain with an eagle on his arm. All the same, he was modestly covered by a wool robe. It felt odd asking him about genitalia.

"Oh," he replied, nonplussed. "They come from the sixteenth-century teachings of the so-called mad saint. The penis is believed to bring good luck and drive away evil spirits."

Go figure.

As we climbed higher into the Himalayas, all houses, even those with penises, disappeared. We now passed only the infrequent dark-gray tents of yak-herding families and their stubborn, giant bovine beasts. The ponies that had been carrying our gear turned back, retreating to lower elevations where they could breathe easy. Up here, only yaks had lungs and hearts adapted to the environment. They now carried everything. It was a delicate dance: yaks struggled at lower altitudes—even having to contend with the possibility of heat exhaustion at temperatures above sixty degrees—and ponies were limited in how high they could carry heavy loads.

A week into the trek, I crawled to the front of our tent. In the first light of dawn, I saw that everything was white. Looking more closely, I discerned large lumpy shapes like fallen snowmen. Our yaks were asleep in the meadow. Buried under the snowfall, their breath billowed into the air. I was relieved. The yaks had escaped the previous evening, their herders searching for them well after nightfall. I headed back to my sleeping bag to wait for the young porter who would soon appear with cups of instant coffee.

Harold woke briefly. I snuggled against him instead of into my own bag, ensuring not an inch of space came between us. I wanted to memorize the feel of his body, intimately familiar after twenty years of marriage. I didn't know how many more such mornings we would have. The white wisps of our breath mingled in the tent as he drifted back to sleep and I listened to the quiet sounds of camp stirring to life. Soft voices. Footsteps heavy in snow. The occasional clang of metal on metal.

Meanwhile, I was preoccupied by one question: was I walking out of here?

It wasn't just the snow that worried me.

Yesterday we had climbed for hours along increasingly steep trails. Ominous clouds gathered as we approached a pass that crested at almost 16,000 feet. It was too windy to rest at the top, so we headed down a steep, narrow trail. My pace was strong, hiking poles in cadence with my stride, weight centered, breathing smooth. I had more or less acclimated to the elevation and was past the headaches, sleeplessness, loss of appetite, and general inertia that had plagued me the first few days. My confidence edged on cockiness: I was in my early fifties, and proud of the fact that I was stronger than I'd ever been.

Despite having mostly acclimated, near the top every step was a challenge. The air was even thinner here, making it again difficult to breathe. It felt like being on another planet, in a different atmosphere—but with nothing between me and it, no suit to protect from the elements, no oxygen tank to make things easy on the lungs. We took our time, moving slowly, deliberately. Not surprisingly, the locals struggled less, while the yaks were oblivious, perfectly at home.

I know because when we began the decline and I glanced back toward the pass, I was relieved to see our yak train following behind. Unfortunately, that's when it happened.

My foot slipped out from under me.

Suddenly I was sliding on my back, before skidding to a halt.

*No big deal*, I thought. *I'll get up, sweep the dirt off my rear, and keep going.*

No sooner did I try to stand, than I was back on my butt. Excruciating pain shot through my left leg.

"Are you OK?"

Harold caught up just in time to see my failed attempt to get back on my feet.

"I'm sure it'll be fine," I said, putting my head between my knees and breathing deeply. "I just need a minute to recover." I desperately wanted it to be true.

But when I put my hand on my ankle, I flinched again from the pain.

"Take off your boot," Harold instructed, kneeling next to me. "Let me take a look."

The rest of the hikers joined us, concerned. My world was shrinking, focused on a small spot in my lower left leg. My ankle had already started swelling. Soon I could barely get it back into the boot. There was no way I was walking.

My mind kept alternating between pain and fear. Options were few. The yaks were out of the question—I had seen their antics, the herders trying desperately to get them under control. The last pony to remain with us was long gone, two thousand feet somewhere below.

As I wondered what to do, Tandin squatted beside me. Unlike the other guides, who resembled a mix of the smaller-framed peoples of Nepal and China, he was tall and large-boned. Given the circumstances, his robust, imposing stature was comforting.

"I will carry you, Tania."

He spoke quietly, with a confidence I didn't expect in someone so young.

"Carry me?" I asked, as though I weren't sure I'd heard right. It was still a four-hour walk to camp. The very idea seemed ludicrous.

I looked around. No one had a better one.

Harold took my things and helped me stand. Tandin moved his daypack to his chest and prepared to lift me onto his back. He held one arm under my left knee so my ankle wouldn't bounce. Finally, he started off, down the mountain, every foot-plant landing firmly, as if we were in Central Park and not on the side of a Himalayan peak. I clung to him like a living, breathing backpack. At first each step was jarring, but soon either the Advil or exhaustion mellowed me out.

For the two hours it took to reach the base of the slope, Tandin entertained me with stories about his childhood. I don't remember the scenery—or much else—but I remember that Tandin played basketball with the crown prince—now king—of Bhutan. That he participated in archery contests. That his father left when Tandin was very young and remained estranged from the family. That his mother lived in the remote village where she was born, although the rest of the family had moved to the capital, Thimphu. And I learned all about Grandfather, the patriarch of his clan and a devout Buddhist. In Bhutan, Tandin explained, it is the husband who moves in with his wife's family, rather than the other way around, as in China and India. Grandfather had six daughters, and he had to provide housing for all their families.

After a long descent, we reached the horse we had hoped would carry me for the rest of the trek.

It had no saddle. There was no way for me to ride it.

Tandin would have to carry me for another two hours, all the way to camp.

First though, he needed a well-earned break. He carefully lowered me onto a large rock.

I passed out.

---

By evening, my ankle had swollen far beyond the size of my boots. Our medicine kit consisted of Advil and arnica gel. I had never heard of the latter.

"It's a special healing cream. It reduces swelling," my friend Jean explained, as she sat on Harold's cot in our tent. "I never go anywhere without it. Can I put some on your ankle? I'm sure it will make it feel better."

The very thought of anyone touching my ankle was nearly unbearable. But Jean warmed her hands, spread the cream evenly on them, and then, as if coddling a newborn baby, gently caressed every inch from my toes to my knees.

She performed that ritual three times a day. By the second evening, the swelling had reduced so much that my ankle was nearly normal. I was convinced arnica gel was a miracle medicine.

---

Just after dawn on our second morning at camp, the porter arrived, calling "Hello sir!" as always.

That meant me. Everyone was "sir." In his usual flip-flops, he stood in the snow outside the tent and poured steaming-hot liquid into a banged-up metal cup. At that moment, it was more exquisite to me than the finest China.

We had already spent an unplanned extra day here. Stuck between two major mountain passes, we had no radio signal and no way to call for a helicopter. The nearest road was a many-day walk away, and we were less than halfway through one of the most challenging trips in Bhutan.

After the coffee, washing, and packing, Harold lifted me out of the breakfast tent and helped me onto a rock. Jean gave me a final rub of arnica. I then put on a thick pair of socks and eased into my heavy leather boots. I tied the laces firmly enough to hold my foot steady. Harold and Jean each gripped me under an arm and helped me stand. Jean's husband Yves and the rest of the group stood in a broad circle. A lot was riding on this moment.

Slowly, I put weight onto my left foot, as everyone watched with bated breath. I was barely aware of them. All my concentration was on my thigh muscle, on carefully lowering my knee, on the toe of my boot touching the ground.

Excruciating pain tore through my body. I screamed, obliterating the silence. Tears streamed down my face. Harold and Jean held on tightly, making sure I was supported. I shifted my weight to my good leg, desperate to do anything but give up.

I looked at Yves, the organizer of the expedition. Lean, medium height, with sharp features and dark hair, he looked the part of a stereotypical Frenchman. Having served in the Foreign Legion in Algeria, he was tough—and suffered no wimps. I remembered our first meeting a few months earlier. He had wanted to make sure Harold and I were prepared, and I had to convince him that six months and two weeks after my ACL surgery I would be ready for the trek. I had told him I was as tough as he was.

Now I had to prove it. And not just for my sake. I was as determined to continue for Harold as for myself, since we never knew how much longer he would be walking.

I breathed deeply, looked Harold in the eyes as he wiped my face, and said: "I can do this."

Harold turned to the others and asked for a moment alone. They walked away, no doubt considering contingency plans.

We sat down. Harold caressed my hand, waiting until I was calm.

"You know we can figure something out," he said, "some way to get out of here."

"No, Harold, it's really OK. I can do this."

"Baby, are you thinking about me or yourself?"

I just looked at him, not even understanding the question. After years fighting the same enemy day in and day out, our relationship always viewed in the context of it, Harold and his illness and I had merged into a single entity. There wasn't a *him* or an *it* different from *me*. There was just us, a precious and unbreakable whole.

"I'll do it, sweetheart. Really."

That single first step, that moment of pain, had somehow exorcized the unendurable. Or perhaps it showed me what I was up against, setting my expectations, so I could muster the will and stamina to tackle the challenge. I had always believed I had a high pain tolerance.

That belief was about to be tested.

I will never know how I did it—how I continued hiking on an ankle I later confirmed was broken. What I do know is that for the next twenty days my only medication was Advil and the thrice-daily, ritualistic application of arnica gel, a medicine I have never been without since.

We weren't on a relaxing stroll. Most of the time we were above fourteen thousand feet of elevation. We crossed three more high passes—all of them higher than the tallest mountain in the United States.

A cultural trait of the Bhutanese people is their inability to say anything negative. No matter how often we asked, the guides replied that the destination was "not too much farther," even though some days we hiked for more than fourteen hours. Our longest day ended in a blinding snowstorm; the next morning we woke to two feet of snow. Level surfaces did not exist; we were either climbing or descending. Some of our fellow travelers came close to giving up, but I saw no choice but to persist. Through it all, Tandin was never far from my side.

Some days after my fall, Harold and I sat alone on a boulder above the trail. We had just passed wild sheep clambering on the rocks. I leaned between his open knees, feeling the warmth of his chest and taking in the breathtaking mountain view. To experience moments like these was why we always pushed ourselves to the limit instead of sitting on a beach in a fancy resort. I lost myself in daydreams until his words brought me back.

"Tania," he said, "we should have Tandin come to school in California, maybe live with us."

"That sounds lovely," I said, "but do you think we can handle something like that? I thought we wanted to be free, you know, to do stuff."

"Of course I still want that, but something in me also wants to do something for him. If it wasn't for Tandin…" His voice dropped off. "I don't know where we would be right now. Don't tell me you haven't been thinking the same thing."

I had been. After all these years together, that happened often.

"Do you think you'd have the energy to work with him?" I asked.

"Even if I don't, it would still be a great opportunity. Besides, you've always had enough drive for both of us."

It was an old joke between us, but I suspected he was right. Besides, like many things that can't be explained, this idea just felt natural. We would let it evolve.

Near the end of the trek, Tandin led us through remote villages that might as well have been stuck in the Middle Ages. Behind sensuously curved, golden fields of rice, rose forests capped by snow-covered peaks. In one field, a young woman stood atop a large pile of rice sheaves, bunches of stems that had been bound together after being reaped by hand. Her round face was topped with a cap of black hair. She wore a long skirt with a rich violet print and a bold brocade jacket over a green blouse. She stared, curious.

When Tandin came into view, she smiled—as everyone always did upon meeting him. The other villagers gathered around, smiling, laughing, and joking. He played with the children, flirted with the young women, teased the grandmothers. Even the dogs came to play with him.

"Do you know these people?" Harold asked, mystified.

"Oh, no." Tandin clarified. "I've never been here before."

But he had been in similar places. Thoughts of his mother's farm and village were often on Tandin's mind as we walked through this final leg of the trek.

---

"Tandin," Harold asked one afternoon, as we walked through a forest where orchids grew from tree trunks, "what would you think of going to college in America?"

As I tended to do even in those days, I had been hanging back, entranced. Now we all looked at each other. We knew it was an important moment.

"Oh… That would be amazing, but I do not believe I would qualify," Tandin replied, each word carefully considered. "My grades were not so great, and my test scores are not high. And I could not afford it without a scholarship."

Despite his reservations, we could see the desire in his eyes.

By the time we reached Thimphu—which became the country's new capital in 1961, when a group of villages in the valley formed by the Wang Chhu river were combined—we were anxious to meet Tandin's grandfather. We had heard so much about him, and we wanted his blessing on our plans for Tandin.

The room where the meeting was held was dim, light filtering in from two rows of windows, panes framed in carved wood. The walls were divided into gold panels, with religious tapestries hanging alongside photographs of monks in traditional robes. The room had a chest, a couple of simple tables, and some pillows with elaborate, colorful designs. Along with a few of Tandin's aunts and cousins, we sat on floor mats, yak-butter tea before us in unadorned ceramic cups. A hint of incense lingered on the air.

Listening closely, Grandfather didn't say much. Slight of stature, with wrinkles like the bark of a tree, he was slim and straight as the bamboo arrows he had shot in his youth. His eyes sparkled, and he smiled easily, exuding a calm dignity and strength. His gnarled fingers never stopped moving over his prayer beads.

Even seated, Harold towered over everyone else in the room. Still, he seemed the supplicant as he explained our idea.

Grandfather eventually spoke.

"I understand how my family might benefit from your offer," Tandin translated. "I understand how Tandin might benefit."

Here Tandin paused, as if concerned about what came next. Finally, he looked at Harold and me, then continued.

"But how do you benefit from bringing my grandson to America and sending him to college?"

Everyone stared at Harold—Tandin with trepidation, Grandfather inscrutably, the others with curiosity. Harold, while fighting for his life since the cancer diagnosis, had developed a wisdom that could still surprise me.

"I am a relatively new student of Buddhism," he began, "but I like what it teaches about releasing goodness into the universe and seeing how it circles, perhaps returning when you don't expect it."

Grandfather's face broke into a grin we hadn't seen until now. I knew Harold and I had just been accepted into his extended family.

Tandin and Grandfather exchanged a few words. Then Tandin turned to us, chagrined.

"Grandfather wants you to know I have not always been a model student. Or the most obedient son."

"Tell him we already figured that out," I replied with a smile.

Tandin let out a laugh, followed by a sigh of relief, his shoulders dropping as his body relaxed. We agreed to set up an email account for him, and he would use the computer at a café in town to communicate with us.

Harold and I left Bhutan believing we would soon have a student in our household again.

---

A lot changed in the aftermath of the comparatively innocent days when we'd hiked the Himalayas with Tandin. The 9/11 terrorist attacks eliminated any possibility of the United States granting him a visa to study in California. A scholar heading for Stanford or Harvard, maybe. A young man hoping to enroll at Santa Rosa Junior College, no way. After extensive exchanges with congressmen and consulates and colleges, we hit a dead end.

While Harold and I struggled to come up with an alternative, Tandin was accepted to a college in Bangkok.

After consultation with his family, we agreed to send him there to study computer science.

At first he sent regular updates; then, in the second year, communication dropped off. Tandin was half the world away. It was hard to be closely involved, to help. Less than eighteen months into it, we learned he had failed out of the program. He was simply unsuited for it. But we heard nothing from him.

Were we pouring money down a rathole or supporting a promising young man, someone struggling but worth our continued commitment? Was Tandin likely to stay connected with two people in far-off America? Or had he already disappeared for good?

We might have given up more easily if we hadn't gone through something similar with our own son. Brad had struggled through school, yet eventually earned two master's degrees. Whenever he ran into problems, he retreated and became hard to communicate with. We knew this scenario intimately. So, rather than cut our risks by cutting off Tandin, we clung to our faith that he would eventually find his way.

When Tandin realized we weren't giving up on him, he found another program. It would let him work year-round and finish in three years.

"You won't regret this. I promise you," he emailed.

In just over four years, Tandin graduated from Bangkok University with a bachelor's degree in Hospitality and Tourism Management. By then he had also fallen in love with Chhimi, a fellow student from Bhutan. Although Harold wasn't well enough to attend the graduation ceremony, he always kept the announcement tucked with family photographs.

While friends and family spoke at Harold's memorial, in a small temple in Thimphu, Tandin lit one hundred eight yak-butter oil lamps to ease Harold's passing into his next life. Tandin wanted me to come and do the same.

Three years later I did.

In many ways the trip was a homecoming. I flew to a country still familiar, yet modernizing rapidly, with construction underway everywhere. Tandin's aunt had just passed, and we spent days with monks, family, and friends, observing their traditions of mourning and remembrance. I sat for hours listening to mesmerizing chanting that brought Harold back for me with surprising ease and clarity.

Grandfather was older and more frail, but no less welcoming. When I asked if he would let me record his praying, he pulled me close, his voice rising and falling in a prayer he had probably performed millions of times.

One afternoon Tandin and I went to the small temple near the family home, where a monk took us into a special altar room filled with rows of yak-butter lamps, like Christian votive candles. Tandin and the monk left me alone and, with soft chanting in the background, I lit one hundred eight lamps. At first, it seemed an enormous task. But as I neared the last lamp, I slowed down. It felt as if Harold were there with me. I wished I could light one hundred eight more.

Or maybe never stop.

Sloane Square was announced long before I ran out of memories of Bhutan. Leaving behind the peaceful Himalaya of my mind for the frenzied city outside the train, I began the ascent to the square.

Walking up the Underground stairs, I found myself troubled by a particular aspect of my memories of Harold; specifically, something that was always glaringly absent.

His face.

I could describe Harold's appearance, remember things he did, recall words he had said. But I couldn't see him—and hadn't been able to since he died. From the moment I learned of his passing until this very one, I had been unable to recall from memory my beloved's visage. No matter how hard I tried, his image was nowhere to be found.

It first dawned on me mere days after he was gone. With a start I was snapped out of my ruminations: I could no longer recollect his face. I panicked. Where was it? How could I lose something so precious, something ostensibly forever ingrained in my mind? It was unfathomable. Yet it was true.

Part of it was intentional: Harold as he had been during the cruel, final days of his illness was not the Harold I wanted to remember. I vowed to banish that Harold from my memory, a way to protect myself, choosing instead to *feel* him as he was—is—spiritually. In the process, I inadvertently banished all of the other Harolds as well, something it hadn't occurred to me was even possible. As pure as my intentions might have been, I had gone too far.

I shook my head, once more giving up the effort. There was no fighting it. I couldn't will Harold's image back into my memory. His face had been forever erased from it.

Walking by full bike racks and a floral kiosk closed

for the night, I left behind the sheltered confines of the Underground. Assaulted by the sounds of heels clicking on sidewalks and horns honking in the distance and a waft of putrid air belched from a trash can, I turned in the direction of the hotel.

My walk along the Thames Path was over.

# Part Three: After the Walk

# A House is Not a Home

I thought I had made considerable progress dealing with Harold's passing. The deep depression that hit me on my return home suggested otherwise.

*Tuesday, March 9, 2012*
*4:30 a.m.*

*I officially announce that I am LOST.*

*Not lost in the sense that I can't find my way home.*

*LOST in the sense that I can't even imagine what HOME means to me.*

*When I was young, HOME was where my parents were. I fought, I resisted, I raged to break away, but it was there. I had a place in it, and I was loved. No matter how far away I went, there was an invisible tie, a super bungee cord that linked me back, kept me from going over the edge.*

*Slowly Harold evolved into HOME, ever deeper over thirty-five years. Ours became a bond of unquestionable strength. We loved and lived and fought. I was never lonely, no matter how far I went, because I was at HOME in my life with Harold.*

*I still have HOUSES, but they are just frames for a life yet to become mine.*

*HOME is what I need to create, to define, to find. HOME for this phase of my life. HOME because my soul needs a place to live.*

*I can't read these words without crying, but a deep joy accompanies the sadness. A joy in all I have in my life: family, friends, resources, health, a strong will. But most of all, joy in my passion for the question, the quest, the search. That is the passion for life that will keep me fighting and living.*

*I believe that of all the gifts I have been given, the most important in this life—itself a mystery—is the desire, against all obstacles, to see what is around the next bend.*

*Because after one of those bends I will realize that I am again HOME.*

I was sappy and sentimental even when journaling. Fortunately, I couldn't bear to look on the negative side of things for long before my determined optimism kicked in, refusing to let me dwell in the dark abyss of depression. My inner self would not tolerate it.

I wrote the words above at my condo in San Francisco. As bad as I was feeling then and there, it wasn't until I headed to the country house Harold and I shared for almost twenty-five years that I tanked.

I started feeling anxious on the drive up. On one hand, I had made the trip so many times, I could practically do it on autopilot, without thinking. On the other, I did think. I thought about the fact that this was not in fact just another drive. At the end of this familiar jaunt up Highway 101 I wouldn't find the life that had always awaited me there. I wouldn't find the man. I wished I could just keep driving, never arrive at my destination.

An hour and a half later, I pulled up to the gate to our property. My property. As I watched it open, the car idling, a black-and-blue scrub jay startled to flight with a shrill squawk, a hole opened up in my stomach. I wanted to turn around and rush back to the city, as fast as I could.

Instead, I meandered up the long, curved driveway. I didn't notice the California-golden grasses or the verdant canopy shading the way or the smell of eucalyptus wafting through the windows. I was too focused on not recalling a desperate voicemail, on not reliving my panicked, unsuccessful rush to get back to the house before Harold was gone.

The house came into view. The front door. The kitchen window looking onto the driveway. The garage. I parked and got out of the car, the pungent scent of bay trees invigorating, as though offering support as I again found myself in a confounding limbo. It was all so familiar, I almost could have convinced myself nothing had changed. But everything had.

I took a deep breath, opened the front door, and stepped inside.

Everything was unnaturally still, inconceivably quiet, as though the house, like me, were holding its breath. I went to turn on the lights, then stopped myself. Better that the interior remain dim. Any more light might have been blinding. My heart growing heavy, a lump forming in my throat; already, looking around was painful enough.

I could not bear this, coming home to an empty house. For so many years it had been filled with our lives, filled to overflowing. How could it suddenly be empty? How was it even possible? It shouldn't be.

Hesitant, as though unsure what I might find, like a stranger in my own home I began wandering around. I thought of the countless mornings Harold and I had shared at the kitchen table, so many cups of coffee I could practically smell their rich aroma. My gaze turning to the living room, I saw his armchair, imagined him sitting there. Reading. Listening to opera. Laughing. God how I missed his laugh.

Not even noticing the beautiful view through the windows—redwoods just outside, rolling hills and black oaks and blue sky farther off, quintessential Northern California landscape as far as the eye could see—I looked at the couch, the other chairs, the big heavy table in the dining room. I wondered how I had ever liked them. Any of them. If I ever had, I didn't now. Not anymore.

# Just Say Yes

As I was about to learn, the same was true for boards.

I went to a couple of meetings and felt about as at home there as I did in my house. After all of the talk with Sharon and Linda about the joys of boards and the opportunities and prestige that came with them, I might have been expected to rejoin mine with renewed enthusiasm. They easily could have provided me purpose and direction as I charted my new path forward.

Instead, as I sat in meeting after meeting, rather than the thrill of debate, the satisfaction of reaching consensus and making things happen, all I heard was a bunch of bickering. I heard people whining and hair-splitting and grandstanding. It was intolerable. Where I had once felt perfectly in my element, found a constructive outlet for my talents and aspirations, I was now fed up. This was not what I wanted my life to be about. Not anymore.

I resigned from all the boards.

In the process, I came up with a new motto: No obligations.

Those two words were about to lead to many more.

Whereas before I had written whenever I happened to feel compelled to do so, now I began starting every morning by writing. Sometimes just a few words. Sometimes more. All that mattered was that I wrote something. Each day.

This wasn't my first attempt to pursue the written word—I had started years earlier with my ill-fated mystery about the scared prostitute in the Tenderloin. This time, however, I found my stride, fueled in part by my desire to chronicle my Thames experience and further encouraged when I discovered a woman who sent out a writing prompt each morning. Getting into a routine helped me stick with it. Soon I was filling pages.

When I realized I could benefit from learning about craft, I signed up for a class. I joined a group called Left Coast Writers at Book Passage bookstore, where I also attended a travel writing and photography conference. I joined a second writing group, where we critiqued each other's works in progress.

My creative pursuits weren't limited to putting pen to paper. I started going on trips with Nevada Weir, a National Geographic photographer with a mad passion for capturing images of people in the remotest corners of the globe. Trips and workshops with other photographers followed.

In the process, I learned that through creativity and travel I could connect with people all over the world. One after another I threw myself into situations where I didn't know what to expect. I went to places few, if any, of my friends or family had been—places whose safety they often questioned. When Harold died, facing the unknown seemed overwhelming; now I not only sought but relished it.

Slowly I found myself rebuilding my life one day at a time, one opportunity at a time, one "yes" at a time. That was the best approach to moving forward.

I just said "yes."

I was amused to realize that, more and more, changes in my body reflected the changes in my life. After a few months, I traded wardrobes with my friend Lynne. She had gained a new man and ten pounds; I had lost mine along with fifteen pounds. I liked the slim new me, and Lynne's clothes were more sophisticated than the outdoor wear I had sported until then.

My mother, too, would have approved.

---

I doubt that Mama understood how much her criticism affected me. She always wanted me to look better. I should lose some weight. I should wear nicer clothes, including the ones she painstakingly sewed for me, using patterns taken straight from the pages of *Vogue*.

It wasn't until I was an adult experimenting with group therapy—a new concept at the time—that I acknowledged I'd spent my whole life ashamed of my looks. I had always felt ugly, primarily because of my mother's constant criticism.

My therapy group insisted I confront her.

At the time I was living in Minnesota. I decided I would talk to Mama on my next trip back to San Francisco.

Several weeks later, we were sitting face-to-face at her kitchen table. I breathed in the fortifying aroma of coffee rising from two porcelain cups, as though it might afford me strength.

"Mother, I need to ask you something," I began,

steadying my voice. She looked at me expectantly, her hand on her cup, immobile. I took a deep breath, my mind swimming, my pulse racing, unsure I would find the words I needed to say next.

I took another deep breath.

"I want you to stop criticizing me."

Her perplexed, wordless expression said it all.

She had no idea what I was talking about.

"I don't want you telling me I'm too fat or unattractive or anything like that anymore," I declared, emboldened now that I'd gotten beyond my initial trepidation.

"Tania, I can't believe you would say that," she retorted, her face betraying disbelief bordering on shock. "I don't think you're unattractive!"

"Thanks Mama, but..." I began, before she interrupted.

"It's just that sometimes you could do more with your hair or wear high heels instead of those boring flats."

After enduring a few more unsolicited suggestions, I doubled down, asking her to never comment on my appearance again. No more criticism. No more ostensible compliments. I didn't want to hear it. Not another word. Ever.

Tears streaming down her cheeks, she promised.

And from that moment forward, she stayed true to her vow.

I never felt ugly again.

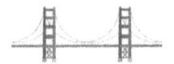

---

After the identity swap with Lynne, I was on a roll. I had my eyebrows and eyeliner tattooed, experimented with hairstyles and colors, and bought my first pair of heels in more than thirty years. I'd like to say wearing them was like riding a bike—but it felt more like walking on stilts. The first couple of outings I was lucky not to sprain an ankle or break my neck.

When I was invited to a Halloween party, not only did I say yes, but I decided to wear my mother's first ball gown, which she had lovingly crafted when we arrived in America. It was one of her few possessions I saved.

At the party, the tall, slim woman wearing a long wig, floor-length black voile, heavy make-up, and fake fingernails didn't get so much as a glimmer of recognition. My appearance was too far removed from my friends' conception of me.

I loved it. I teased people who tried—and failed—to figure out who I was. I laughed when I overheard people wondering about the identity of the mystery woman—me! I even flirted, batting my long, thick, fake eyelashes and playing coy. I hadn't had so much fun in ages, reveling in the unexpected freedom that came with becoming someone else.

I left the party without revealing my identity. I chuckled to myself about it for weeks, before finally confessing the truth.

One day not long after, it hit me. I no longer felt the need to struggle, to figure out who I was and what I was going to do. Rather than stumble upon some cut-and-dry answer, it was organically taking form over time. I could simply let unfold "my one wild and precious life," as the poet Mary Oliver calls it in one of Harold's favorite poems, piece by piece.

Yes by yes.

# Two is Better than One

What unfolded next was a new home.

In late summer 2012, my realtor-turned-friend, Liliana, shared that Gordon's wife had passed away. Gordon had died a few years earlier, so their apartment was likely to go on the market. I was interested.

As soon as the unit become available, Liliana and I went to see it. The windows were dirty, and the place was a mess, filled with old-fashioned furniture. It hadn't been touched for months, left in limbo while the estate was sorted. I wandered through the chaos, before stumbling upon something that made me catch my breath.

"That table was in our apartment!" I exclaimed. My surprise was that much greater, given that this was not the unit we had rented.

I touched the table. The familiar scratch from the earthquake was still there, right where I remembered it.

"And that's the broken chandelier!" I added, looking up. "I can't believe it's here—and still broken—all these years later!"

Liliana followed me deeper into the apartment. Her round face framed by dark hair, the smile normally lighting up her face went dim as she commented how much work this dated mess needed to be put on the market.

I wasn't listening. Instead, I was fixated on something else. Unable to help myself, I burst into tears.

"What's wrong?" Liliana asked, following my eyes but

seeing nothing unusual.

"The desk!" I mumbled.

"The desk?" She repeated, walking over to a small chinoiserie piece centered in one of the floor-to-ceiling windows. "What about it?"

I approached the beautiful furnishing. I lovingly ran my hands over its scratched leather surface. I pulled the drawer out, as though looking for something. My tears turned to sobs.

"Tania, what's wrong?"

"Harold got me this desk when we were first married, when we bought our first house in Minnesota."

I recalled the wedding, a simple affair in Minneapolis. Twenty-five close family and friends joined us in a small restaurant on Lake Harriet.

Presiding over the ceremony was a woman judge—a rare breed back then. She was surprised when Harold and I insisted on not including "until death do us part" in our vows. Why would we? Neither of us could imagine calling to mind our final step as husband and wife just as we were taking the very first. We wanted all of the focus on what we hoped was merely the beginning of a long, meaningful life together. Once we explained our thinking, the judge was won wholeheartedly over to the idea.

Before the big day, Harold and I moved to a nearby hotel, so that our respective families could stay in our house—and get to know each other. A risky tactic, but one that paid off: Harold and I returned to discover that our fathers were already working together on a home-improvement project. One of the upstairs rooms no longer had a ceiling.

The gates now open, all the rest came flooding back:

the early days of our marriage; my study and the views of the lake; my parents and his visiting unexpectedly at the same time; the kids running in the yard in summer; cross country skiing in winter.

The apartment offered birds-eye views of the Marina Green and the deep, white-capped blue of the Bay. A little further off, the Golden Gate Bridge glowed in the late-afternoon light. I didn't notice any of it. I couldn't take my eyes or hands off this desk, this repository of so many memories.

"What's it doing here?" asked Liliana, interrupting my thoughts.

"I gave it to Gordon."

"What do you mean you gave it to Gordon?"

"He'd always admired it. So, when we left the apartment and had nowhere to put the desk, I offered it to him. He was thrilled."

Liliana just shook her head.

If I needed a sign, I now had one.

Just like its predecessor several floors down, I soon owned the apartment.

My new home both linked me to my past and moved me forward. It had a connection to my marriage, but it wasn't the same condo Harold and I had shared. It was wholly mine, a launchpad for my new life.

*If I'm lucky*, I thought, as I walked inside for my first visit as owner, *someday in this very apartment, I'll be ninety-two, watching the sun set behind the bridge, talking about the good 'ole days, and telling jokes to the grandkids.*

I could see a future here.

# Epilogue

I drifted out of some vague dream, my eyes opening to a dark room. Through the windows, I saw the lights of a freighter entering the bay. Even now—sleep interrupted, as it so often was—I reveled in the sight. Looking farther out, I saw mist enshrouding a red bridge, glowing as if lit by the moon behind it.

The room was cool, so I snuggled back under the warmth of my silky down comforter. Luxuriating in the vast space of my queen-size bed, I waited for sleep to come for me again.

Someone else showed up instead.

"God damn it, you're a fucking ghost!" I heard a voice say—a voice that sounded a lot like my own. "You're not real. I know you're dead. Get out of my bedroom!"

I must have dosed off. But I felt awake. If this was a dream—*it had to be, didn't it?*—it treaded a space very near reality.

"Wow! You never talked like that when I was alive."

I tried to push him out. He kept coming back.

"I'm too old for this…this "

"You? You're young. You'll never be too old. For anything."

"Maybe in heaven you don't age," I retorted, "but some of us are still here on Earth."

He caressed me gently. He wrapped his tall body around mine, the feeling as familiar as unsettling—he had been gone for several years. And this man seemed different somehow, almost younger than the one in my mind. Virile. Healthy. Hard.

"Well," he continued, sensual, "your body still feels good."

"Ha!" I said. "Remember how you used to stand in front of the mirror and look at the wrinkles on your arm in disgust? And I would just laugh as I combed my hair? Well now that's me in front of the mirror. Don't give me that 'young' bullshit."

"You'd feel young again if you just let me—"

"I'm not listening to this! If you're going to visit, don't torment me." I pulled the comforter over my eyes, as though it might somehow protect me.

"Don't you remember how much you used to love it when I—"

"No!"

"I don't believe you."

"Well, you should. Besides, I have my eye on someone else now."

"That sap? You can do better."

"Ha! You try and be me. See what that feels like. See who shows up."

"Honey, I'm better than that guy. You know it. C'mon, let's go. Come with me, let's play like we used to—"

"Just go away!"

I rolled over, half asleep, half awake, as the light outside took on the first hues of dawn. I could have willed myself to wake up fully, but something kept pulling me back. No, not some*thing*. Some*one*. The elusive, alluring, frustrating man I had been married to for thirty years. The one who still had a hold on my heart, even as friends suggested it might be time to open myself to the possibility of someone new.

"It's your fault I'm not meeting anyone. I just keep comparing them to you. They're not tall enough. They're not successful enough. Their paunch is too big. They don't have a sense of adventure. I don't like their smile. It's all your fucking fault!"

"There you go with that language again. I like it. It's sexy."

"I thought there were nubile young maidens in heaven. What are you doing talking dirty to a sixty-five-year-old bag?"

"Well, that's your own fault. I just can't stop thinking about you. About us. About before I was sick."

"Oh? You too?"

Before he was sick. The mere mention disarmed me, a rush of memories breaching my defenses.

"Remember that bed we destroyed the first time we made love?"

"How could I forget!" he laughed. "That old Victorian thing you bought at a garage sale after school then carted around the world with you? It wasn't exactly seductive."

"That didn't stop you from making the moves."

"Or you from enjoying it," he retorted, before wondering, "How come you're acting so cold? That's not the way I remember you."

"I've had time to cool off. No beautiful maidens or slick studs hang around my bedroom. Do I have to keep reminding you that life goes on?"

"Come on, let's play," he entreated, ignoring my bitterness. "What do you have to lose? Remember when I used to touch you here... And here... Like this?"

"Go away. You're not real—you're a fucking ghost!"

"Yeah, well maybe a ghost could be fun!"

I said nothing. The truth, after all, was that it was fun.

"Okay," I hesitated, acquiescing, the temptation too great. "Maybe a little more."

He came back the next night. And the next.

It all felt new and exciting, like the first times we were together. His nimble fingers reclaimed terrain they had once known intimately but that had long since become no-man's-land.

"I think you don't want me to find someone else," I ventured.

"Who me?"

"Yes, you," I replied.

Always you.

# Memorial Talk
Harold Thomas Hahn
6/26/2011

Harold was a man who embraced life completely. He was on an endless quest for learning, for experiencing, for challenging himself to be all he could.

By the time Harold was diagnosed with cancer in 1995, when he was fifty-five, he had lived a full life. He had retired from a very successful business career; he had two wonderful children, Brad and Beth, whom he loved passionately; he lived in a beautiful home with this grand redwood grove; and he had many friends. He was a skier, a backpacker, a bicycle rider, a world traveler.

And yet...

And yet, the best part of his life was still ahead of him.

His cancer was aggressive, and the outlook was not good. The treatment caused increasing levels of tiredness and increasingly challenging side effects.

And yet...

In a pattern that would continue for years, he lived fully and in the moment. The first year he spent two months in Vail near Brad and Beth, skiing with friends while I wrapped up my career. We then spent a month trekking around Annapurna in the Himalayas with Bruce and Pam; being in shape, we raced from Yosemite Valley up to the top of Half Dome in one day. We backpacked in Escalante, Utah, with fourteen friends, then drove straight to the Grand Canyon for another backpacking trip down to the

Colorado river.

We went to Africa to see the animals with Bob and Ann, and, by the way, climbed Mt. Kenya.

We spent time in Colorado in the summers and winters, and, lest there be dull moments, we invented a "great cities" program for early Decembers. We got hooked on Paris and that became our "great city" for years to come.

One time a stay in Lee and Nancy's apartment made us miss the commencement of a new treatment program for Harold. When we finally came home, it was to learn that the cancer had gone into temporary remission—one of many miracles that fed our years.

We devoured Italy, spending over a month a year there, falling in love with Camogli on the coast near Genoa and Verona and the Dolomites in the north.

Everywhere we went we met and learned about local people. I would often pick up the language and Harold would quiz people through me, learning about their lives.

In 1998 for a month we rented a house with fourteen beds on Lago Maggiore in Northern Italy. Every bed was taken with our family and friends. Ruth and Barry, Alex and Renée, and my mother Zora were there. Amazingly, Brad and Beth both came with new romantic interests—Sloan and Emily—and Harold had time to fall in love with his future son-in-law and daughter-in-law. The bond with Sloan was such that he and Beth asked Harold to perform their wedding ceremony.

To greet the new millennium, we trained for a marathon. Here at home Harold became a passionate bike rider, teaming with his gentle giants Fred and Dennis.

For his sixtieth birthday, I took Harold helicopter-skiing. I broke my ACL and gave up skiing. Harold found a new love and heli-skiied with Tom and Bob every year after that.

And then the grandchildren came. The first one on the scene was sweet Stella; then Spiderman Baker, born a few weeks later; and, after a two-year break, lovely Miss Sadie. Finally, our captivating Alice, who, although last, was in such a hurry that she was born on the way to the hospital. Dear Harold, who incredibly still wasn't sure he was a good father, became beloved Papa, who read stories to them in our magical aerie above Sonoma county.

As the treatments got tougher, so did Harold. We trekked the Himalayas again, in Bhutan, where he met Tandin and decided to support his education. Amazingly, Tandin just wrote to say his new daughter was born within days of Harold's death.

In 2003 we decided to climb Mt. Whitney. My cousin Nenad from Croatia came to join us, as did Bob Fosberg and my brother, Alex. Harold and I trained by climbing Mt. Tamalpais from ocean to peak and back down—only to realize that was just 2,600 feet of elevation gain. So, we turned around immediately and did it again. We scared ourselves to death that summer training in the Dolomites, but Mt. Whitney was tame after that. (What really scared us was the sight of daughter Beth climbing Dolomite walls we wouldn't go near, five months pregnant with Stella in her belly!)

We trekked in the Dolomites many times. On our final trip there, in 2007, we met "Harold's harem"—the women he hiked with regularly—the two Barbaras, Mary Anne, and Lynne—in the middle of a trek. Sharon and Graham joined us from London.

Harold had another strong group of women in his

life by then—his cancer group, who met monthly for many years of support.

By late 2007 Harold's cancer had metastasized, and he was put on bone-strengthening medication. He was no longer skiing and mostly stopped biking. The first bone treatment had such severe side effects that he was decked for three weeks. One day he could finally get out of bed; three days later we went on a long-planned trip to Patagonia and the Atacama Desert and had a wonderful time. That winter we trekked through the Sahara in Morocco with two nomads and three camels.

By the next year Harold could no longer play pétanque; he stopped going to his discussion group because it was hard to concentrate. He couldn't work with Don at the Riverkeeper. Groups of people tired him out.

And yet…

And yet, he kept reinventing himself.

We had dinner in the City one night at Quince. The owner loved quince and said: "It's a little-appreciated fruit that takes a long time and a lot of work to prepare; the result is subtle, but all the more satisfying for it."

And so, knowing we could no longer trek the Himalayas, we named 2009 our "year of the quince." It wasn't too bad. We went to the beach in Mexico for a week with the family. We spent Easter in Barcelona with Lee and Nancy. We went to Alaska with Judy and Rick to visit the grizzly bears and fly into Denali. We celebrated Harold's seventieth birthday with a magical cruise with friends and sister-in-law Renée on the Nile in Egypt.

The next year Jay and Karen (Harold's angel) flew us to Utah, where we wandered around the Garden of the Gods.

Harold developed his meditation practice and started philosophical readings with Steve and Devaki. He completed his oral course in great music about a month ago—having borrowed a boom box from Mike and Erica when his long-out-of-date cassette player broke down. He continued Pilates with Conna Lee to the last. He spent time with Alex, Al, Bill, Henry, Michael, and other friends, just talking. He walked the path around the property and to his beloved redwood grove several times a day. He made s'mores for the grandkids at night here in the grove.

Harold was a wonderful husband. He insisted that we both live in recognition of how fragile life could be. Through everything, he encouraged me to have a full life and loved to hear stories of my independent adventures. He was my best photography critic. He was my behind-the-scenes advisor on PSST.

He served me coffee in bed every morning until the end.

We had an amazing life together.

Harold's aggressively physical lifestyle, I believe, prevented the cancer from destroying his bones. He died as he wished, peacefully, with no bone pain, at home and surrounded by family and friends.

He didn't just beat the negatives cancer tried to offer. Harold's victory was his life, a life well and fully lived.

Harold loved opera, and one of his favorite arias was "Nessun dorma" from *Turandot*. It is the song of a prince determined to win. The final word, *vincerò*—I will win—might have been Harold's.

I have no doubts—he did win.

# About the Authors

**Tania Romanov Amochaev** is the author of *Mother Tongue: A Saga of Three Generations of Balkan Women* (Travelers' Tales, 2018), also published in Serbian as *Po Našemu* (Akadems Kaknjiga, 2020); *Never a Stranger* (Solificatio, 2019), a collection of award-winning travel essays; *One Hundred Years of Exile: A Romanov's Search for Her Father's Russia* (Travelers' Tales, 2020), published in Russia as СТО ЛЕТ ИЗГНАНИЯ (Rosspen Publishers, 2021) and winner of Gold for Memoir in the Northern California Publishers and Authors Book Awards; and *San Francisco Pilgrimage* (Solificatio, 2022). Tania's work has been featured in multiple travel anthologies, including *The Best Travel Writing* and *The Best Women's Travel Writing* series. Born in the former Yugoslavia, Tania spent her childhood in a refugee camp in Italy, before emigrating to the United States, where she grew up in San Francisco's Russian community. A graduate of San Francisco public schools, she went on to serve as CEO of three technology companies.

taniaromanov.com

Matthew Félix is the author of four books, a certified life coach, and a speaker. *Publishers Weekly* called his debut novel, *A Voice Beyond Reason*, "(a) highly crafted gem;" his *With Open Arms* was an Amazon Hot New Release and topped its Africa category; and, his most recent book, *Porcelain Travels*, was a Foreword INDIES Humor Book of the Year finalist. The former host of the San Francisco Writers Conference Podcast, Matthew regularly conducts interviews at San Francisco Bay Area bookstores and cultural institutions. He also ghost-writes, edits, designs, publishes, and markets books for other authors.

matthewfelix.com

Printed in the USA
CPSIA information can be obtained
at www.ICGtesting.com
JSHW080348061124
73054JS00001B/2

9 798985 878158